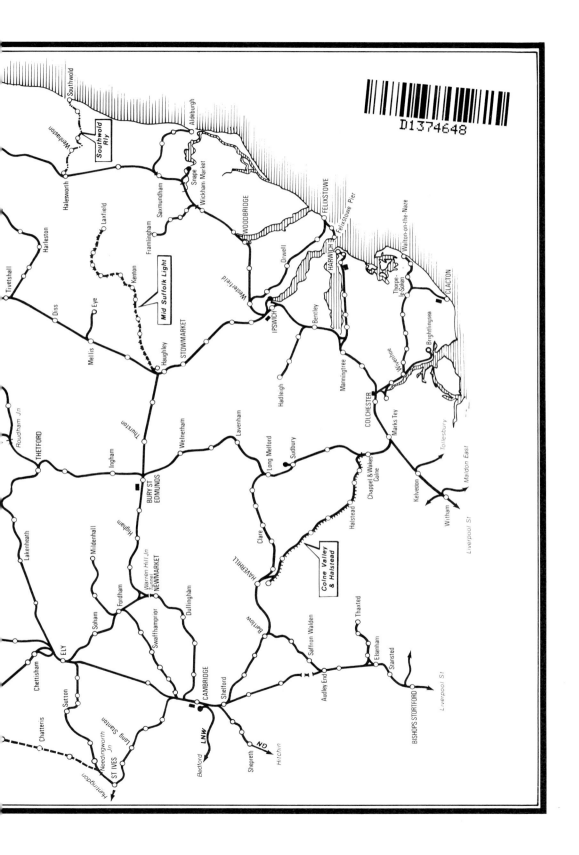

STEAM
IN THE
EASTERN
COUNTIES

STEAM
IN THE
EASTERN
COUNTIES

John Brodribb

LONDON

IAN ALLAN LTD

First published 1985

ISBN 0 7110 1558 9

© Ian Allan Ltd 1985

Published by Ian Allan Ltd, Shepperton, Surrey;
and printed by Ian Allan Printing Ltd at their works
at Coombelands in Runnymede, England.

Cover:
Class B17/6 No 61664 *Liverpool*
**leaves Yarmouth with the
15.14 departure to Liverpool Street
in April 1957.**
E. Alger/Colour-Rail

Preface

his book is an attempt to give a picture of railways in ast Anglia in the years following World War 2, until e end of steam. I have tried to give an impression of e levels of service that might have been encountered y the traveller, although train times and frequencies aried over the years. I have relied heavily on public d working timetables, and any errors in their terpretation are entirely mine. It seemed a relatively raightforward exercise to arrange the photographs d text in a logical order – until I started it! There ere so many connecting lines and alternative routes at it was remarkably difficult: they are roughly in the der Marks Tey to Cromer; Elsenham to Hunstanton; d the Midland and Great Northern lines; with equent diversions along branches and secondary utes.

Apart from the timetables mentioned I have referred numbers of books to check particular items of formation, and they are also invaluable for anyone terested in pursuing the historical aspects of local ilways. A list is appended, but it is by no means clusive.

A number of people have been extremely helpful, tably A. W. Godfrey, Arthur Hadingham, Russell hipps and J. R. Besley; many people have also been ry kind in allowing me to look at and use otographs, notably A. T. Jarvis, E. Cotton, H. N. mes, A. R. J. Frost and A. J. Willmott. I am tremely grateful to all of these, and to the many hers who have helped, sometimes unwittingly! If any ader can throw any additional light on any of the aterial herein, or correct any error that may have ept in, I'd greatly appreciate knowing it.

It is worth noting that there are several places where the steam era lives on in East Anglia. The North Norfolk Railway at Sheringham, the Colne Valley Railway at Castle Hedingham, the Stour Valley Railway at Chappel & Wakes Colne, and Bressingham Gardens near Diss all offer the real thing puffing up and down. Wolferton station museum is well worth a visit, and so is the North Woolwich station museum, although the latter is hardly in East Anglia. There is also the transport museum at Carlton Colville, near Lowestoft. Many smaller places have their own museums which very often have railway exhibits, and Southwold is a notable example of this. Much can still be seen on the existing network, and the book *East Anglia by Rail* is an invaluable guide when used in conjunction with the British Rail timetables and Ordnance Survey maps. Finally, no account of East Anglia and its railways is complete without mention of the M&GN Circle and the Great Eastern Society, whose efforts to record, collate and disseminate historical information are wholly admirable.

Principal Reference Books

Forgotten Railways: East Anglia, R. S. Joby, David & Charles.

The Great Eastern Railway, Cecil J. Allen, Ian Allan Ltd.

A Regional History of the Railways of Great Britain: Vol 5 – The Eastern Counties, D. I. Gordon, David & Charles.

Pre-Grouping Atlas and Gazetteer, 5th Edition, Ian Allan Ltd.

Steam in East Anglia

In the late 1940s and early 1950s the pattern of railways in East Anglia remained very similar to that of prewar years, and indeed to that of the pre-grouping era. They seem to have had a long and difficult birth in the area, and the Eastern Counties Railway was particularly maligned for its discomfort and poor time-keeping. Early rivalries left their mark, and the traveller to Norwich to this day has to suffer the sharp curves and speed restrictions which were needed to allow Eastern Union trains into the Eastern Counties station at Thorpe. The latter had originally refused such access, which necessitated construction of a separate terminus at Victoria. This closed to passengers as early as 22 May 1916, but most of the branch remains for coal traffic.

In 1862 almost all of the existing railways in East Anglia were amalgamated into the Great Eastern – in effect, an enlarged Eastern Counties, which then held sway over most of the area. This situation was not to last, and a series of small local lines, mostly in Norfolk, were promoted and built and eventually amalgamated into the Eastern & Midlands Railway. When this concern ran into severe financial difficulties it was taken over as a joint enterprise by the Midland and Great Northern companies, which had long harboured desires to tap East Anglian traffic, and the Midland & Great Northern Joint Railway was born. Although it provided the Great Eastern with its only real competition in the area, two other lines were later built as a joint venture under the title of the 'Norfolk & Suffolk Joint Committee'; the lines were from Lowestoft to Yarmouth via Gorleston, and North Walsham to Mundesley and Cromer.

The Great Eastern duly became part of the London & North Eastern Railway at the grouping in 1923, and although the M&GN remained a joint concern between the LMS and LNER, the latter took over completely in 1936. Even so, the 'Joint' retained its identity to the last, and in spite of its almost total elimination from the railway system of today, many traces can still be found. Indeed, the discerning traveller can still see remnants of the Great Eastern and its predecessors, even on lines that have been electrified for many years.

The two principal Great Eastern lines in East Anglia started at the cavernous and smoky Liverpool Street station in the City of London, and connected it to Cambridge, Ely and King's Lynn, and to Colchester, Ipswich and Norwich. From all of these radiated secondary lines, many served by through trains or coaches. The main line to Yarmouth was the East Suffolk via Beccles, where trains divided regularly, one portion going forward to Lowestoft and the main part on to Yarmouth South Town. Unlike today's InterCity services, which run almost exclusively

between, say, Norwich and London, express train often started or finished on the secondary line: Hunstanton, Sheringham, Yarmouth and Lowestoft a had direct services. Additionally there were als through trains from places like Lowestoft an Yarmouth to the Midlands and North, many via th M&GN.

There was also a variety of cross-country route which had been developed over the years, and whic provided a number of valuable links, most importar on summer Saturdays. The lines from Norwich to El and from Haughley Junction to Ely and Cambridg remain, but additionally one could travel fror Norwich to King's Lynn via Dereham and Swaffham or between Colchester and Cambridge via Sudbury an Haverhill. Trains from the Midlands to Clacto worked via Bury St Edmunds and Long Melford t Marks Tey. There were the archetypal rural branc lines to Mildenhall, Aldeburgh, Framlingham an others, and the splendidly-isolated Mid-Suffolk lin from Haughley to Laxfield. Many of these lines ha been built and operated on a shoestring over the years and were early victims of closure.

The railways were still major carriers of freight i the late 1940s and 1950s. Most local stations including ones like those on the Hadleigh branch wit no passenger service, had at least one visit daily fror the stopping goods train, which took an almos interminable time en route because of the need to shur every station and siding. Their time-keeping was ofte not helped by their lowly position in the classificatio of trains, which were then lettered from A to K i descending order of precedence: freight, mineral o ballast trains stopping at intermediate stations wer Class K.

In East Anglia local freight traffic included th ubiquitous coal – every yard had its own merchant and agricultural goods. There were heavy season flows of fish, especially from ports such as Lowestof and sugar-beet during the autumn campaign. In spite o the technological wizardry of places such a Whitemoor Yard at March, horses still shunted a many stations such as Woodbridge, in Suffolk.

The railways were very labour intensive. In th postwar period railwaymen enjoyed benefits an working conditions won for them by their Unions ove many years, although it was not to be long before th encroachment of road transport forced drastic change in the railway industry. Country stations were stil fully staffed in the postwar years: for instance in 195 Beccles had a stationmaster, three lorry drivers, seve shunters, three guards, three ticket collectors, tw leading porters, four porters, nine signalmen and on relief signalman, as well as five men in the good department; then there were crossing keepers, engine crews for the four locomotives based there, and so on. There were many more lines open, most of them with a full complement of signalboxes and level crossings. Provision of the latter had reduced initial costs of many lines, the landscape being relatively flat, but the price was exacted later in the cost of crossing-keepers, which militated against many branches. Large stations, with their locomotive depots, had correspondingly more staff, with engine crews, cleaners, fitters, carriage and wagon examiners and many more. Then there were the permanent way men. The local gang would have its own section of line, its length being governed by the number of running tracks, sidings and so on. Before the advent of mechanisation it was heavy work, much of it moving ballast with pick and shovel, and one of the least glamourous departments of the railway. It was also one in which great pride was shown, and many lines had their 'Prize Length'. These men might be called out in fog or falling snow to place detonators on the rails to give drivers an indication of the aspect of signals they could not see; to be 'fogging' at night in freezing temperatures gives real meaning to the term 'unsocial hours'.

There was the other side of the coin, of course. Many railwaymen were keen gardeners and their stations won prizes for their displays; many a fine crop of tomatoes has been raised in country signalboxes. There was a real sense of pride and community among railway staff, born of a long tradition of stability and public service. By the end of the 1960s the country branch line in this sense was extinct, a victim of the all-conquering motor car and motor lorry.

Most journeys from London to East Anglia started from Liverpool Street station. The Great Eastern Railway had been renowned for its intensive steam-worked suburban services to places such as Chingford, Enfield and Leyton, and although electrification began to encroach in the 1950s, steam haulage persisted for several years over the longer distances. The Great Eastern section received the first of the powerful new 'Britannia' class locomotives in 1951, having already had some of the Southern's Bulleid Pacifics on trial. The 'Britannias' revolutionised passenger workings, and for a time the Great Eastern main line boasted the fastest schedules anywhere in the country!

Trains for the main line to Norwich generally left from Platforms 7 to 12 at Liverpool Street. The exit from the station remains slow and tortuous, as trains thread their way through the station throat and tackle the gloomy climb past the remains of Bishopsgate station, the line's original terminus. At Bethnal Green – a major junction where the Cambridge lines diverge and the gradient eases – more tracks become available. Long distance trains such as the Yarmouth or Sheringham expresses didn't usually stop until Chelmsford, and several made no pause until Colchester. Only one missed all of these and Ipswich

Above:
Looking across to the steps up to the Bishopsgate exits the bustle of the station even at quiet periods is obvious. It is no surprise to learn that this photograph was taken to illustrate the advantages of advertising at the station.

as well, and that was the 'Easterling', a summer-only service to Yarmouth South Town and Lowestoft, which made its first and only intermediate stop at Beccles. This was also the only regular named train over the East Suffolk Line.

Once past Shenfield, the junction for Southend Victoria, the main line was down to double track. Chelmsford was a major traffic centre, but the station imposed operating restrictions. It was approached from the London side over a long curving viaduct, and there was a speed limit over this and through the station. The goods yard was at the Colchester end of the layout, which was approached by a steeply-graded connection, the main line still being on an embankment. After the line to Shenfield was electrified in 1949 a regular-interval service was introduced between there and London, and Chelmsford was provided with a steam-operated connecting service. The Clacton interval expresses generally called there, as did many of the longer distance trains. This gave a best time of about 43 minutes from London, later reduced to 38 minutes for some of the 'Britannia'-hauled limited load expresses. Chelmsford was thus provided with a weekday service of at least one express every hour, with locals in between.

For several years the 'Britannias' reigned over the Great Eastern, ably assisted by the older 4-6-0s – 'B1s', 'B12s' and 'B17s', the latter introduced in 1928

Below:
'Britannia' class No 70039 *Sir Christopher Wren* is ready to leave on a Sunday in April 1958 with the 8.24am for Norwich.

Bottom:
A panoramic view of the country end of the station is full of activity on 14 June 1958. The Pindar Street bridge is in the foreground and Broad Street station approaches in the background. At Liverpool Street the following can clearly be seen, from left to right: D202 on the 10.30am to Norwich; coaches of the 'Broadsman' about to leave as empty stock; Class B17 No 61647 *Helmingham Hall* on the 10.44am to Clacton; Class B1 No 61283 waits to go 'on shed'; the up 'Butlin Express' runs in behind a 'Britannia'; and the 10.47am Clacton waits with a BR Standard Class 4.
British Transport Advertising/Brian Morrison/R. E. Vincent

nd known as 'Sandringhams' after the first of the lass. In the 1950s the 'Britannias' were allowed just nder the hour to pass Colchester non-stop from iverpool Street with nine coaches, reaching Ipswich a a best time of 76 minutes. The Pacifics usually orked right through to Norwich, but they were often ken off Yarmouth trains at Ipswich and replaced by a -6-0. Unlike the present day, a great many express ains continued beyond Norwich, usually to Cromer, heringham or Melton Constable. The 'Norfolkman', hich left London at 9.30am, ran fast to Ipswich and orwich and on to North Walsham, whence the main ortion with restaurant car worked forward to Cromer igh. The remainder was taken via Mundesley and the orfolk & Suffolk Joint line to Sheringham. The Broadsman', which left Liverpool Street at 3.30pm, ffered a similar service, and thus places like rimingham and Overstrand had a regular daily service and from London, taking just over three hours each ay. This finished in April 1953 when the line etween Mundesley and Roughton Road Junction losed to all traffic. Mundesley then became the rminus of a branch, normally with a service to and om North Walsham, but with some trains to and from orwich Thorpe.

There were many other lines which branched from e main Colchester to Norwich route. At Marks Tey, ve miles on the London side of Colchester, the ross-country route from Cambridge joined the main ne. The junction faced the Cambridge direction and as thus convenient for through running from olchester. There were five or six trains daily in each irection over the line via Sudbury, and some of them ere divided at Chappel & Wakes Colne, one portion

going via the Colne Valley line to Haverhill, and the other via the Stour Valley. The route saw a great variety of motive power, ranging from the veteran Class E4 2-4-0s introduced by the Great Eastern in 1891, through the even older 'J15' 0-6-0s to 'Claud Hamilton' 4-4-0s, 'B1s' and ex-LMS Ivatt Class 2s. Further variations were provided by the freight trains. Apart from the usual Class K workings there were regular trips to Whitemoor Yard, March, which were sometimes handled by ex-War Department 2-8-0s.

Long Melford, the next station to the north of Sudbury, was the junction for Bury St Edmunds. This branch saw a passenger service of some four or five trains daily, and was used for excursions and through workings to Clacton and Walton in the summer; it also saw some of the heavy freight from Whitemoor. The line was unusual in being one of the last haunts of the ex-Great Northern Class C12 4-4-2 tank locomotives.

Returning to the main line, Colchester itself was a major traffic centre and junction. The main station, Colchester North, remains some way from the town centre, and while St Botolphs is much more conveniently sited, its position at the apex of a triangle off the line to Clacton and Walton has made it awkward operationally, and served only by local trains. Some of the major expresses such as the 'East Anglian' did not call at Colchester, but for many more it was the first stop out of Liverpool Street. A service of buffet car expresses ran between Clacton and London, and conveyed coaches for Walton. There were five such workings in the 1951 winter timetable, which were later expanded to form the 'Clacton Interval Service' of buffet-car trains which were about hourly throughout the day between 6.00am and 8.00pm. The best-known of this group was the 'Essex Coast Express', which called only at Thorpe-le-Soken en route for London. Clacton also received a great many trains from various places on summer Saturdays, most of which had a Walton portion.

The Brightlingsea branch, known locally as the 'Crab and Winkle', remained a rural by-way until the end of its life. It was served by trains from Wivenhoe, several of which started from St Botolphs, and with an occasional through working from Colchester North. The branch was single track throughout and was latterly the haunt of 'J15s' hauling two or three coaches. The typical service was about 11 trains each weekday, with extras on Saturdays; there were three Sunday workings. The branch was dieselised relatively early, which brought about a distinct improvement in the number of trains – up to about 14 daily – although this lasted only until closure in June 1964. The branch had already survived the floods of 1953, much of it being washed away, but it was rebuilt and re-opened in December of that year.

There were two other branches between Colchester and Ipswich, of rather different status. The line to Harwich diverged at Manningtree, where a triangular junction allowed through running from both directions,

and was originally built to serve Harwich and Dovercourt. The Great Eastern Railway reclaimed a great deal of land between Wrabness and Dovercourt and constructed a new port, together with railway station and goods yards. The branch was diverted to serve the new installation, which was called Parkeston after the then-Chairman of the GER, Charles H. Parkes; the original trackbed can still be seen. As a result of its port status, fast named trains connected Harwich and Parkeston Quay with Liverpool Street, usually conveying only 'Passengers holding tickets to or from the Continent', and such celebrated names as the 'Day Continental' and the 'Hook Continental' survive to this day. These trains would often run in several parts: for instance, in the summer of 1957 the 'Hook Continental' was booked to leave Liverpool Street at 8.00pm, with a second part at 8.10pm and reliefs 'as required' at 7.40pm, 8.13pm and 8.47pm. Only the main train was advertised in the public timetable, and carried a restaurant car. An additional advertised train was provided at 8.20pm on Wednesdays and Fridays. Booked times varied between 90 minutes for the main train to 105 minutes for the 7.40pm relief; none but the 8.13pm relief (which called at Colchester) had any intermediate stops. The terminus for these trains was either Parkeston or Parkeston Quay West. There were other through trains from London such as the 5.45pm, which survived for several years, but in general, ordinary passengers had to change at Manningtree, although some branch trains worked to and from Colchester. Another notable daily working – forerunner of today's 'European' – was to and from Liverpool Central,

which left in the morning at about 8.00am and returned at about 9.00pm.

Goods traffic was varied in the days before the container boom and usually arrived in the form of Class D or E partly-fitted freight, or Class H from Goodmayes, Spitalfields or Whitemoor. One or two pick-up trips sufficed for the local station traffic on the branch, although there were a number of trips between Parkeston and Harwich, and numbers of light engine workings. Mistley Quay was served by a short steeply-inclined branch from the main line at the Harwich end of the station, and a special 12-ton brake van was kept for working it. Strict limits were placed on the numbers of wagons which could be worked over the incline, although descent by gravity was permitted provided that the brake van was the leading vehicle and the maximum load was eight wagons. Even in the 1970s though, provision was still made in the Local Instructions for vehicles to be hauled up by horse power!

The Hadleigh branch, just over seven miles long, joined the main line at Bentley, and lost its passenger service on 29 February 1932 in the first round of railway cuts. Bentley had been planned as a triangular junction, but only the southern half was built, which permitted through running from the Colchester irection only. The freight service outlasted the assenger by 33 years, and in the mid-1950s there ere still two trips daily from Mondays to Fridays. In ne morning the Class K goods would leave Ipswich, ause for about half an hour at Bentley, where it eversed, and then leave for the 45-minute journey to Iadleigh, calling at Capel and Raydon Wood as equired. After spending just over an hour at the erminus, the train left for Bentley, where it spent nother hour before leaving for Manningtree, calling at Keebles Siding on the way. After a stay of some two ours at Manningtree, the train returned to Bentley and Iadleigh in a similarly leisurely fashion, finally eturning to Ipswich just over 10 hours after leaving.

Ipswich was and is an important centre for both reight and passenger services, and sports one of East Anglia's few tunnels. In steam days, down trains used ne two faces of the island platform, numbers 3 and 4, vith the main train running in on number 3, and onnecting services at number 4. For Felixstowe, it vas usually necessary to cross over the footbridge to Platform 1, a bay at the Norwich end of the main up latform, number 2. The station area was controlled by wo signalboxes, Ipswich Station on the London end of ne down platform, and Ipswich Goods Junction, about quarter of a mile north, between the down main and elief lines. The Griffin Wharf branch, a freight-only ne, diverged south of the tunnel at Halifax Junction, vhich was dignified only by a small ground frame.

This junction had been necessitated many years before, when the railway was extended past the then-station, through the tunnel, and into the present station. The site of the original station was taken over later by the locomotive depot. To the north, another goods line ran down to the Upper and Lower Yards, and since it crossed the River Orwell, gave access to the quays on the other side of the river. Ipswich had an allocation of tram engines, which were needed because the quay branches ran through the streets in places. It was home to a wide variety of motive power, ranging from the Class E4 2-4-0s and 'J15' 0-6-0s of the Great Eastern, through the 4-6-0s such as Gresley's 'Sandringhams' to Thompson's powerful Class L1 tanks used on the Felixstowe services. The Pacifics were never allocated to Ipswich, always being based at Stratford or Norwich, although they were a very familiar sight, of course. Ipswich carriage sidings were easy to see, being immediately adjacent to the down platforms, and could usually be relied on for some sort of activity.

Below:
Ipswich Lower Yard is seen from the Princes Street bridge in April 1952, with Class J67 No 68518 engaged in shunting operations. This yard was reached down an incline from the Upper Yard, and also gave access to the quay lines on the other side of the river. *A. R. J. Frost*

Strange though it may seem to today's passenger, the East Suffolk line was once the major through route between Great Yarmouth and London, and carried a regular service of express and local trains, as well as heavy freight traffic. In addition there were various junctions and branches along its length. The passenger for Lowestoft or Yarmouth might have been fortunate enough to catch an express from Liverpool Street, such as the 3.33pm shown in the 1957 winter timetable. Its exact timings varied over the years, but it was then booked to call at Ipswich, Saxmundham, Beccles and Yarmouth South Town. It conveyed through carriages for Felixstowe Beach, and was divided again at Beccles, the rear portion being worked forward to Lowestoft. Felixstowe then had only two through workings from London, and one in the other direction. There were two expresses from South Town to Liverpool Street, but four going the other way, most conveying buffet cars. In 1959 the weekday summer service was four down and six up buffet car expresses, although the line was about to be truncated with the closure of the Beccles to Yarmouth section. There was a service of stopping trains between Ipswich and Yarmouth, and most of these also detached a portion at Beccles for Lowestoft. The procedure for this movement was for the train to run into the down main platform, and for the Lowestoft coaches, at the rear, to be uncoupled. The Yarmouth train would then hurry away, having paused for about five minutes, after which a Lowestoft-based tank engine, often a Class F4 or F5 2-4-2, then backed on to the remainder. The thirsty passenger just about had time for a beer in the hotel outside the station while all this was going on!

In the reverse direction the Lowestoft coaches arrived first on one side of the island platform, and the locomotive would be uncoupled and run forward. The Yarmouth coaches would then arrive at the other face of the up platform and the train locomotive would uncouple, run forward and set back on to the waiting Lowestoft portion. It then transferred them on to the front of the Yarmouth train, and the whole would then leave. About 11 minutes were allowed for this. A local service of 'motor trains' (push-pull or auto-trains) operated between Yarmouth and Beccles, calling at all stations, and a few of these ran through to Saxmundham. Until 3 January 1953 passengers could travel along the meandering Waveney Valley line from Beccles to Bungay, Harleston and Tivetshall Junction which had about six return trips a day, several to or from Norwich.

The East Suffolk crossed the Norwich to Lowestoft line at Haddiscoe, and although there was a single track link between Fleet and Haddiscoe Junctions no regular passenger services ran over it. However, some slick connections could be made between the high and low-level stations by passengers travelling from Norwich to, say, Halesworth. The link was used for excursion traffic – such as when Norwich City played Ipswich Town – for newspaper trains, and was a useful

Below:
On 21 April 1954, Class B1 No 61253 has just restarted the 12.10pm Yarmouth South Town to Liverpool Street from Haddiscoe high level station. *R. E. Vincent*

iversionary route. Freight services over the East Suffolk used the line, since the goods station at Haddiscoe was on the low level. Haddiscoe Junction signalbox is now preserved in the Science Museum in London.

Halesworth had once been the point of exchange with the narrow-gauge Southwold Railway which closed in 1929, and until 1941 it was possible to see the derelict remains adjacent to the main line station. Saxmundham was the junction for the Aldeburgh branch, which had about six passenger trains each way on weekdays, often hauled by 'J15s'. A little further south, Snape Junction saw some of the fastest running on the East Suffolk; it was the junction for the short branch to Snape. This was always freight-only, and trains ran as required.

At Wickham Market Junction, about a mile north of the station, the Framlingham branch joined the main line. Again, it lost its regular passenger service relatively early, in November 1952; prior to that it had enjoyed four return trips on weekdays, with no Sunday service. It did see excursion traffic until its final closure in 1965, much of it in connection with Framlingham College, although it was the freight traffic that kept it open.

The East Suffolk was a line built largely at minimal cost, and followed the undulations of the countryside. With the introduction of the 'Britannia' Pacifics, the Norwich to Ipswich line services were accelerated to a much greater extent than was possible on the East Suffolk, and in spite of the latter's shorter route it became faster to travel from Yarmouth Vauxhall to London via Norwich than from South Town to London via Beccles. The direct route was severed on 2 November 1959 with closure between Beccles and South Town, although the section from Haddiscoe to Aldeby remained until 1965 for freight, mainly sugar beet. Some Yarmouth to London trains were diverted to run from South Town to Lowestoft via Gorleston, especially on summer Saturdays, but the extra time, distance and the reversal at Lowestoft ensured that they had a relatively short life.

Leaving Ipswich, the main line to Norwich swung in a northwesterly direction, a legacy of its origins. It started as the Ipswich & Bury Railway, and took a fairly direct course between these places. Stowmarket, about 10 miles from Ipswich, had a good service to and from London, and most of the Norwich expresses called there. Ipswich to Cambridge trains also stopped, and these often also served the other smaller stations, including Haughley Junction where the Norwich and Cambridge lines diverged. There was also a stopping service between Norwich and Ipswich of about five or six trains daily, although some of the expresses did call at some of the lesser places.

Haughley was also the junction for the Mid-Suffolk Light Railway, which meandered through very pleasant countryside to Laxfield. It had once had grandiose ambitions to reach Halesworth, and the first

sod was actually turned at Westerfield on another doomed branch to Kenton, halfway along the line. The up and down morning trains were booked to run as mixed workings, and there was a freight on Mondays, Wednesdays and Fridays. For a short time before closure the afternoon train started from Stowmarket, for the benefit of school-children. The end came on 26 July 1952, and it was lifted the following year.

Continuing along the main line to Norwich the station at Mellis had a service in winter 1951 of six down trains daily, two of which were through from London; indeed the 1.30pm was a buffet car express to Cromer High. At one time passengers could have changed there for the Eye branch, about 2¾ miles long, and which survived for freight until 13 July 1964, although the passenger service had been withdrawn on 2 February 1931. The daily freight on the branch left Norwich Thorpe at 3.15am, and reached Mellis at 8.33am, a distance of 23½ miles being covered in just five hours! Naturally it had called at all stations on the way. Leaving Mellis about an hour later, it then took about 15 minutes to reach Eye, whence it returned after about 45 minutes. It then proceeded to Stowmarket, calling at all stations – in this case, at Finningham and Haughley. This was the only all-stations freight working over the Norwich to Stowmarket section, although the 6.05am Ipswich to Norwich Trowse covered most of the stations from Stowmarket to Tivetshall.

Diss, on the main line, had a good service with many expresses calling. Just over five miles further on was Tivetshall Junction, where the Waveney Valley line from Beccles converged. After withdrawal of the passenger service over the latter in 1953, freight continued for some time. The line was closed between Harleston and Bungay in 1960, and thereafter worked from each end, as had been done in practice earlier. The stubs were progressively cut back until final closure in 1966.

The next station on from Tivetshall was Forncett, which had also been a junction at one time. Trains could run from the London direction to Wymondham, and then on to Dereham and Wells. The usual optimistic hopes of the promoters failed to be realised, and passenger services were withdrawn in 1939. An interesting working before final closure in 1951 had been a regular freight trip from Beccles, along the Waveney Valley, and thence via Forncett and Wymondham to Wells, which provided a very full day for one of the locomotives shedded at Beccles.

Norwich itself was a complex place for railways. It had once boasted three termini, although Victoria closed in 1916 and was only built as a result of intransigence by the Eastern Counties Railway, which would not let the Eastern Union Railway – which built the Haughley to Norwich line – use its station at Thorpe. When agreement was finally reached, a link was constructed between Trowse Upper and Lower Junctions, which, coupled with the severe speed restrictions over Trowse Swing Bridge and Thorpe Junction, have always bedevilled operations in and out of Norwich. A 'Britannia'-hauled express could dash as far as Trowse Upper from Ipswich at well over a mile-a-minute and still need almost four minutes to cover the remaining two miles into the terminus.

At Thorpe Junction the line from Lowestoft, Yarmouth and Cromer converged, all services normally going into Thorpe station, but the Wensum curve formed the third side of the triangle and allowed certain trains to avoid the station. These were mostly holiday expresses from the Midlands and North, working through to the coastal resorts on summer Saturdays; many had travelled over routes such as the former Great Northern and Great Eastern Joint line via Spalding and March. The curve assumed more importance for a short time after the closure of the Midland & Great Northern Joint lines in 1959, but was finally taken out of use in 1982 to make way for the servicing depot at Crown Point. Local services from Thorpe, apart from those to Ipswich, included those to Lowestoft via Reedham; Yarmouth Vauxhall via Reedham and also via Acle; and to Cromer and Sheringham. Lowestoft enjoyed about 14 trains a day by this route, with at least two through from Peterborough East, and a through working to Birmingham and York. Summer Saturdays saw the usual increase; local services were considerably augmented when diesel multiple-units were introduced. Yarmouth Vauxhall received nearly 30 trains daily, and similarly had through workings from Peterborough, York and Birmingham. With closure of the line between Yarmouth South Town and Beccles, expresses were introduced to London from Vauxhall; in the winter of 1964/65 there were still four each way daily. This service has now also almost disappeared. Local services northward from Norwich were principally to Cromer and Sheringham. Apart from the expresses already mentioned, about six trains daily called at all stations to Cromer High, via North Walsham. Most continued to Sheringham, and in order to do this they had to reverse back to Cromer Junction and take the curve to Roughton Road Junction, where they joined the Norfolk & Suffolk Joint line from Mundesley. This practice was discontinued in 1954 when Cromer High was closed to passengers – it was very inconveniently sited high above the town, a mile from the centre. All trains then ran into the former M&GN station at Cromer Beach, having to reverse there to reach Sheringham.

Another interesting route was from Wroxham to County School. Trains worked from Norwich to Dereham by this route, and it was possible to get back to Norwich via Wymondham simply by staying on the same train! The passenger service was another early casualty, closing on 18 September 1952, which left Aylsham served only via the M&GN line as regards passenger trains. The line from Reepham to Foulsham was lifted early in 1957, but a daily goods trip along

the truncated branch from Wroxham survived f[...] several years. The section from Reepham [...] Thelmelthorpe, where the line had crossed the M&G[...] branch from Melton Constable to Norwich City, w[...] reinstated in 1960 after the latter had closed [...] passengers, in order to give access to that line witho[...] having to work all the way round via Sheringham. T[...] M&GN was then lifted between Thelmelthorpe a[...] Melton Constable; the line thence to Cromer was st[...] open for passengers at that time.

Other services from Norwich ran to Dereha[...] Wells-next-the-Sea (known in LNER and early B[...] days as 'Wells-on-Sea') and King's Lynn. Trains [...] Wells usually stopped at all stations, and took up to 1[...] 50min to cover the 43½ miles. There were about s[...] trains daily, with extras on Saturdays; most connect[...] at Dereham with services to King's Lynn. On the oth[...] hand there were also trains to Norwich from Lynn v[...] Dereham. This offered competition to the M&GN li[...] from Norwich City to South Lynn, and in 1951 sa[...] five trains each way on weekdays, with extras [...] Tuesday and Saturday. As with many lines, the adve[...] of diesel multiple-units brought an improvement [...] service frequency before they succumbed to closure [...] the 1960s: the last Dereham to Wells train ran on [...] October 1964.

The other route out of Norwich Thorpe was, [...] course, to March and Ely, and it gave the Gre[...] Eastern its main link with the Midlands and North, [...] well as offering an alternative route to London. It sa[...] stopping trains between Norwich and Cambridge, [...] well as a variety of through services such as the dai[...] York to Yarmouth and Lowestoft train, which used t[...] GN&GE Joint line from Doncaster to March. The[...] were many extras on Saturdays in the holiday seaso[...] mainly to the seaside resorts. Wymondham was o[...] important junction; Thetford was another. A line we[...] southward through Thetford Bridge, Barnham a[...] Ingham to Bury St Edmunds, and in the early 195[...] supported a service of four passenger trains daily fro[...] Monday to Friday, with an extra on Saturday evenin[...] All except the last one back to Bury on Saturday h[...] connections to or from London. The other route out [...] Thetford was to Swaffham via Roudham Junction. T[...] latter did not appear in the public timetable as a statio[...] but it was used as such by railway staff living in t[...] vicinity. The service was a little better here – fi[...] trains each weekday, with one from Thetford [...] Watton, and a service out from Thetford in t[...] morning and back from Swaffham in the evening f[...] school-children. The service again offered connectio[...] to and from London for most trains, and there we[...] even two Sunday trains in the early 1950s. T[...] Thetford to Bury passenger service closed in 1953, b[...] the Swaffham line lasted into the Beeching er[...] earning the distinction of being claimed as the m[...] uneconomic line in the country in the celebrat[...] 'Reshaping of British Railways' report. It closed f[...] passengers in 1964, and for goods the following ye[...]

One other service which deserves a mention here is that from Wells to Heacham, which saw four return workings a day. There were few places in East Anglia accessible by only a single route, which is a consequence of the flat terrain. Many rural lines such as this one were built cheaply, following the lie of the land, and although it ensured low speeds, level crossings in abundance and an early demise, it gave the area a very reasonable rail network for the carriage of passengers and the staple agricultural produce. As an example, consider a person from Burnham Market travelling to London in 1951. Leaving at 8.14am, it was possible to reach Liverpool Street at 12.37pm, having changed at Heacham, King's Lynn and Ely. Alternatively, by leaving at 9.25am arrival could be made in London at 1.55pm, having changed at Wells and Norwich, catching the 'East Anglian' from the latter. The cost? From Wells to London it was 26s 4d (£1.32p) third-class single, or a monthly return was 35s 4d (177p). The traveller could have taken luncheon for 6s 0d (30p) on the 'East Anglian', although only a buffet car was provided for the journey via King's Lynn, this being available from Ely. Gentlemen could even have a bath at Liverpool Street – at any hour of the day or night – for a mere shilling! Incidentally, there are several interesting entries in the table of fares shown between London and 'Principal Stations' in the 1951 timetable. In East Anglia Wells, Aylsham, Brightlingsea, Hunstanton, Mundesley-on-Sea and Wisbech all qualify for entry: none has had a railway passenger service for many years.

The other major route out of Liverpool Street was the main line through Cambridge and Ely to Norwich and King's Lynn. From the latter one could continue, after reversal, to Hunstanton, a distance of 112 miles from the capital. The route was – and is – an interesting and demanding one to work. Cambridge had eight routes converging on it, and Ely six. King's Lynn could be reached along three former Great Eastern lines, as well as by the Midland & Great Northern routes. The London & North Eastern regarded the London–Ely–Norwich route as the principal one, and this persisted into early British Railways days; however, by the end of the 1950s the position had changed and the main service was diverted to King's Lynn.

In the winter 1951 timetable Cambridge could be reached from Kings Cross by the 'Cambridge Buffet Express' service, of which there were four each way on Mondays to Saturdays. They were popularly known as the 'Beer Trains' and offered a best time of 80 minutes on the 3.10pm up from Cambridge. There was quite a good service of stopping trains on this route, though they were much slower and usually called at all stations between Hitchin and Cambridge. The Buffet Expresses were matched on the Liverpool Street route by the 'Fenman', which did the down journey in 90 minutes, and the up in only 75 minutes. There were quite a number of fast trains between Cambridge and

Liverpool Street, most continuing to Norwich and several having either a restaurant or buffet car. They called at most stations between Ely and Norwich, and so the overall running time could be almost five hours – not competitive with the Ipswich route. March was served by through coaches from some trains, and the 4.36pm from Liverpool Street continued thence to Wisbech. Timings to Cambridge by the fast trains were about 90 minutes depending on the number of stops; most called at Broxbourne, Bishops Stortford and Audley End. Others called at all stations beyond Bishops Stortford, taking two hours for the journey to the University City.

There were many major and minor junctions on the way. Elsenham was very much in the latter group, being where passengers changed for the Elsenham & Thaxted Light Railway. It was built as late as 1913 and survived barely 40 years. At the end it boasted five down passenger trains on Mondays to Fridays with four on Saturdays; there was one extra train daily the other way. All had connections to or from London, and offered a best time of about 1½ hours from Thaxted to Liverpool Street; although since the station was a good mile from the town, this must have been more in practice! Journeys over the 5½-mile branch varied officially from 21 to 29 minutes.

Audley End was more important as the junction for Saffron Walden, and was thus a centre for passenger traffic. The branch went via Saffron Walden and Ashdon Halt to Bartlow, on the Cambridge to Colchester line, although the great majority of trains traversed only the first 1¾ miles from Audley End, taking four minutes for the journey. In 1951 there were 21 trains each way on Mondays to Fridays, of which five ran to or from Bartlow. The first allowed an arrival in London at 8.48am, and the last returned to Saffron Walden at 10.00pm. Branch trains were usually worked on the push-pull principle, latterly using Class N7 0-6-2 tanks displaced by London suburban electrification. They were replaced in 1958 by the four-wheeled rail-buses, without the service frequency being improved. The branch closed for passengers on 7 July 1964, and completely in December of that year.

Shelford, about 11 miles north of Audley End, was the junction for the other route to Bartlow, which continued via the Colne or Stour Valley lines to Marks Tey and Colchester. In practice, trains worked to or from Cambridge, and numbers of cross-country workings ran this way, especially in the summer peaks. The service was otherwise relatively sparse and fairly slow, since trains called at all stations, taking about two hours to cover just over 50 miles.

Less than a mile north of Shelford the line from Hitchin converged at Shepreth Branch Junction, the 'Beer Trains' from Kings Cross arriving this way. Nearer still to Cambridge the former London & North Western line from Bletchley and Oxford made its junction at Trumpington, and it was thus possible to

Above:
**Standard Class 4 No 75037 makes an impressive start from
one of the bay platforms at the south end of Cambridge
station with the 11.20am to Bletchley via Sandy and
Bedford St Johns on 14 September 1957.** *P. J. Reindorp*

see a remarkable variety of locomotives and rolling
stock at Cambridge. The station remains unusual in
having only a single long platform for both up and
down trains, with cross-overs halfway and bays at each
end.

To the north, the line to Newmarket and Bury St
Edmunds diverged almost immediately at Coldham
Lane Junction. This was a main line and Newmarket
was an important traffic centre, especially so on race
days when it would see many specials. On a normal
weekday some local trains called at all stations
between Cambridge and Ipswich, while others omitted
stops to Newmarket, or between Stowmarket and
Ipswich. A couple of trains ran from Ely to Cambridge
via Newmarket, using the curve between Snailwell and
Warren Hill Junctions, and there were local workings
to and from Bury. The line from Ely to Chippenham
Junction was used by a number of cross-country trains,
such as the Glasgow to Colchester, which left the
former at about 9.15pm and arrived at the latter at just
after 11.00am the following day! Another interesting
working was a buffet-car express from Liverpool
Central to Harwich, which worked via Spalding and
March, as did the Glasgow train mentioned above.
Through coaches off the 'Fenman' were detached at
Cambridge and taken on to Bury St Edmunds on
weekdays, and this gave a journey time from the latter
to London of 126 minutes in the up direction, and 135
minutes the other way, the whole procedure being
reversed.

The Mildenhall branch was a classic East Anglia
by-way. Leaving the main line at Barnwell Junction,
wandered across the Fens to Fordham, where it joine
the Chippenham Junction to Ely line. At the other en
of the station it branched off again, reaching
Mildenhall after another seven miles, the total length
being 20¾ miles. In steam days there were three return
passenger workings daily, with timings that scarcel
varied over the years. In 1942 departures from
Cambridge were at 6.40am, 10.28am and 4.27pm
returning from Mildenhall at 7.49am, 11.50am and
6.00pm; all had connections to or from London
Dieselisation brought an extra train each way t
Mildenhall itself, but, except on Saturdays, all but on
return working ran via Newmarket. New and exoti
destinations such as Ely and Marks Tey could be
reached without change of train, but the changes wer
short-lived and the line closed on 18 June 1962.

March could be reached by two routes from
Cambridge: they diverged at Chesterton Junction. Th
main line towards Ely is well-known, and the throug

16

service to March and Wisbech from London has already been mentioned. In the early 1950s it was often necessary to change at Ely if travelling by this route, the local service being run between Ely and Peterborough East. Some through trains were run with coaches detached from Liverpool Street to Norwich workings. Other services between Cambridge and March ran via St Ives, usually calling at all stations and taking just over an hour to travel the 34 miles, slightly slower than the other route. On weekdays, two trains ran via Newmarket to Cambridge, but in steam days there was no corresponding return working. By 1959 some trains had been dieselised, but a variety of other workings had been introduced. On weekdays three trains each way ran between Cambridge and Kettering via St Ives and Huntingdon East, and the 8.07 from Cambridge worked via St Ives to March, and then on to Wisbech, King's Lynn and Hunstanton. In the winter timetable for that year the Hunstanton service was 'rationalised' – in other words through services were generally withdrawn – and the St Ives service simplified. This did not enable it to survive the Beeching cuts.

The town of Wisbech could be reached either via the M&GN, or by the Great Eastern line from March to Magdalen Road. There were three stations bearing the name of the town: North, on the M&GN; East, on the Great Eastern; and Wisbech St Mary, which served the village of that name about 2½ miles west of the town on the M&GN line. The Great Eastern route saw six or seven trains daily, with a handful of extras between March and Wisbech. There were lines to the quays on both banks of the river, Wisbech being an inland port on the Nene. Timber was an important freight traffic, arriving from the Baltic for onward transmission by rail. The town was also served by the Wisbech & Upwell Tramway, which lost its passenger service as early as 1927, but which remained for freight until May 1966. It was celebrated as the haunt of Class Y6 0-4-0 tram engines, and the larger Class J70 0-6-0s, although these were superseded by Drewry diesel shunters during 1952/53, also suitably fitted with cowcatchers and skirts.

Through workings on to the Hunstanton line have already been mentioned, such as those from Wisbech, and of course the 'Fenman'. King's Lynn being a terminus, all of these involved reversal there; some M&GN trains also worked through to the Great Eastern station. In 1951 there were eight trains daily to Hunstanton from Lynn, including the 'Fenman' which did not run on Saturdays. There were 10 in the other direction; additionally there was a Lynn to Heacham train, and two from Wells to Hunstanton, but only one the other way. There was a Sunday service of four trains each way, the last one up missing all intermediate stations except Heacham.

The Midland & Great Northern Joint Railway had provided the only real competition to the Great Eastern Railway in East Anglia, although the two later collaborated in the building of two joint lines under the auspices of the Norfolk & Suffolk Joint Railway Committee. Very little remains today of the M&GN or of the N&S Jt: the only operational parts are from the former Cromer Junction to Cromer Beach, and from there to Sheringham; also the preserved North Norfolk Railway. One legacy of the early rivalry was that many places had two stations: North Walsham Main and Town, Aylsham North and South, Reepham and Whitwell & Reepham are obvious examples. Cromer Beach, Yarmouth Beach and Norwich City were the main termini; M&GN trains used Lowestoft Central. The line provided an important link with the Midlands, and came into its own on summer Saturdays. In winter the service was relatively sparse, although it must be remembered that Norfolk has one of the lowest population densities of any English county, rendering local traffic prospects bleak. In 1951 trains left Yarmouth Beach at 6.51 and 7.45am, the first being all stations to South Lynn, then calling at Sutton Bridge, Wisbech North and Peterborough North, whilst the second was an 'all stations' to Aylsham North. Use of the term stations here is deliberate, and excludes the many 'halts' between Yarmouth and Potter Heigham which were used only in the summer months. There then followed the 'Leicester', which left Lowestoft at 8.15am, and ran via Gorleston and the swing-bridge over Breydon Water to Yarmouth Beach, whence departure was at 9.00am. It then called only at Potter Heigham, Stalham, North Walsham Town, Aylsham North and Melton Constable, where portions from Norwich City and Cromer Beach were attached, only eight minutes being allowed for this. The combined train then called at Fakenham West and South Lynn before going on via Bourne to Leicester London Road and Birmingham New Street, the latter reached after a journey of about 7½ hours from Lowestoft. It took rather less time in the opposite direction, and the journey times corresponded with those of the Great Eastern route.

The 10.05am from Yarmouth went to Peterborough and called at all stations to South Lynn. The 12.0 noon train called at all stations to Stalham and ran on Wednesdays and Saturdays only; the 12.42pm to Peterborough served all stations to Sutton Bridge. The next train to run every weekday was not until the 4.55pm to Melton Constable, which did not run beyond North Walsham on Saturdays; after that the 6.15pm had a connection from Lowestoft and Gorleston, and ran to Melton Constable and Cromer Beach. At Melton there was a connecting train for Lynn at 8.10pm, which ran through from Norwich City, and also connected with the 7.25pm from Cromer. There was a later train from Yarmouth at 9.00pm on Wednesdays and Saturdays, and as with many lines, a late night extra on Saturdays only to Stalham, which left at 10.40pm.

There was no Sunday service, at least in winter, over the main line from Yarmouth to Peterborough or

Bourne, although there was one passenger working from Holt just after mid-day, which called at Weybourne, Sheringham and West Runton, and then reversed into Cromer High before going on to Norwich Thorpe and Liverpool Street. Towards the end of the 1950s this train from Holt became a summer-only working, but another was put on at 4.45pm, which worked via Cromer Beach, Norwich Thorpe and Cambridge to London – rather a long way round.

The branch from Norwich City to Melton had eight passenger trains each weekday in the 1950s, with two extra on Saturdays. There was considerable freight into Norwich, and the concrete works at Lenwade was a source of much traffic. The last portion of this line,

between Lenwade and the curve at Thelmelthorpe, was not lifted until 1984.

Most of the M&GN closed to passengers on 2 March 1959, the only part remaining being from Melton Constable to Cromer. The section between Melton and Sheringham lasted only until 6 April 1964; several parts remained for goods but have now all gone, except where mentioned. Arguments still rage about what was one of the first major closures, mostly along the lines of 'did it fall or was it pushed?'. Whatever the answer, the North Norfolk line from Sheringham to Weybourne is worth a visit, as is the Colne Valley at Castle Hedingham, and the Stour Valley at Chappel & Wakes Colne.

Finally, the two lines of the Norfolk & Suffolk Joint Railway Committee. They were the route between Lowestoft and Yarmouth via Gorleston, and between North Walsham and Cromer via Mundesley. Neither fulfilled the hopes of their promoters, which were to open up the Norfolk and Suffolk coast. Lavishly laid out, the latter had five or six trains each way daily, with the luxury of through portions of both the 'Broadsman' and the 'Norfolkman' to and from London. Freight was sparse, and closure early, on 17 April 1953 between Cromer and Mundesley, although the latter station was served from North Walsham until 5 October 1964. The other line of the Norfolk & Suffolk Joint fared rather better, although Hopton and Corton did not develop as they had been intended to. Except on summer Saturdays, when the holiday camps received a great deal of traffic, there were only about 10 or 11 trains daily, including the 'Leicester'. Some worked from Yarmouth South Town, and others went into Yarmouth Beach, although this practice ceased when Breydon Bridge was closed in 1953. Heavy renewals and upgrading took place after the Beccles to Yarmouth line closed in 1959, and the London to Yarmouth service briefly ran this way. In 1962 these trains were rerouted in to Yarmouth Vauxhall, and the line downgraded shortly after. It finally closed in 1970 to passengers.

East Anglia still has many miles of railway, and a great deal of railway history is there to be seen. With the coming of electrification, it is well worth arming yourself with the appropriate Ordnance Survey maps and local train and bus timetables, and getting out and seeing it first-hand.

Shed Codes in 1959 in East Anglia

30A Stratford, Chelmsford, Enfield Town, Ilford, Wood Street (Walthamstow)
30B Hertford East, Buntingford, Ware
30C Bishop's Stortford
30E Colchester, Braintree, Clacton, Maldon, Walton-on-Naze
30F Parkeston

31A Cambridge, Ely, Huntingdon East, Saffron Walden
31B March, Wisbech
31C King's Lynn, Hunstanton
31D South Lynn
31E Bury St Edmunds, Sudbury
31F Peterborough (former Midland shed)

32A Norwich, Cromer Beach, Dereham, Swaffham, Wymondham
32B Ipswich, Felixstowe Town, Stowmarket
32C Lowestoft
32D Yarmouth South Town
32E Yarmouth Vauxhall
32F Yarmouth Beach
32G Melton Constable, Norwich City

The Classification of Trains

Class A
Express passenger train, or newspaper train, or breakdown van train or snow plough going to clear the line, or light engine going to assist disabled train. Officers' Special train not required to stop in section.

Class B
Ordinary passenger train, or mixed train, or breakdown van train NOT going to clear the line, or loaded rail motor train.
* Branch passenger train.

Class C
Parcels, fish, fruit, horse, livestock, meat, milk, pigeon or perishable train composed entirely of vehicles conforming to coaching stock requirements. Express freight, livestock, perishable or ballast train, pipe fitted throughout, with the automatic brake operative on not less than half the vehicles. Empty coaching stock train (not specially authorised to carry 'A' headcode), or empty rail motor train.

Class D
Express freight, livestock, perishable or ballast train, partly fitted, with the automatic brake operative on not less than one-third of the vehicles.

Class E
Express freight, livestock, perishable or ballast train, partly fitted, with not less than four braked vehicles connected by vacuum pipe to the engine. Express freight, livestock, perishable or ballast train with a limited load of vehicles NOT fitted with continuous brake.

Class F
Express freight, livestock, perishable or ballast train NOT fitted with continuous brake.

Class G
Light engine or light engines coupled. Engine with not more than two brake vans.

Class H
Through freight or ballast train not running under class 'C', 'D', 'E' or 'F' headcode.

Class J
Mineral or empty wagon train.

Class K
Freight, mineral or ballast train stopping at intermediate stations.
* Branch freight train.
Freight, ballast or Officers' Special train requiring to stop in section.

* To be used only where authorised by the Operating Superintendent.

Above:
Marks Tey was the junction between the main line from Liverpool Street to Colchester and the Stour Valley line to Cambridge via Long Melford. Class B17 No 61639 *Norwich City* pulls out with a train for Colchester from the branch platform, now used only by trains to Sudbury.
Real Photographs (K2866)

Below:
This magnificent bracket signal was a feature of Marks Tey station for many years, controlling movements in the down direction from both branch and main. Class J15 No 65456 takes water. *A. J. Willmott*

Above:
Class J39 No 64751 is seen at Colchester on 26 August 1957. The locomotive had been serviced there before heading back to its home shed (Cambridge) on a passenger train, probably via the Stour Valley. The long shed can be seen in the background with various engines standing outside.
John Brodribb collection

Below:
Electrification work began on the Clacton and Walton lines at the end of 1957. The branch was used as a pilot scheme for the then-new 25kV system, and Colchester station was rebuilt at the same time. Class J19 No 64651 is seen coming up off the Clacton line with an engineers' train on 22 April 1958; erection of masts is already well under way.
John Brodribb collection

21

Above:
A busy summer Saturday at Colchester on 15 August 1959. British Railways Class 7 No 70013 *Oliver Cromwell* **heads the 12.38pm from Liverpool Street to Yarmouth South Town via Lowestoft, whilst Class J15 No 65445 is in charge of the 08.03 Birmingham to Clacton. The latter had arrived via Peterborough and Ipswich, and reversed at Colchester.**
Roger Mann

Below:
The same location and date as the previous photograph: Class B1 No 61378, a Colchester engine, hurries the up 'East Anglian' through its home station, deputising for a failed 'Britannia'. In spite of their lower nominal tractive efforts, the 'B1s' put up some very creditable performances when filling-in on 'Britannia' timings: the 'East Anglian' schedule allowed exactly two hours between Liverpool Street and Norwich, with one stop only, at Ipswich.
John Brodribb collection

Above:
St Botolphs station, much nearer the centre of Colchester than the main line North station, was the usual terminus for Brightlingsea trains. 0-6-0 Class J15 No 65424 is seen running in on such a train on 15 February 1957.
John Brodribb collection

Below:
The splendid nameboard leaves little doubt as to the location! Class J15 No 65448 pulls in with a Brightlingsea train, again in April 1949. *Real Photographs (K177)*

Left:
Class J15 No 65448 is ready to leave
Brightlingsea for Wivenhoe in April
1949. The crew have rigged a sheet
between cab and tender – either
they are trying to avoid coal-dust
blowing into the cab, or they are
expecting an April shower.
Real Photographs (K178)

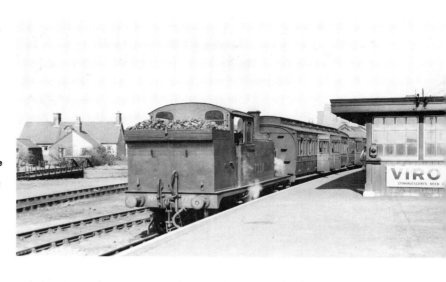

Below left:
Class B2 4-6-0 No 61644 stands at
Thorpe-le-Soken with a train for
Colchester. The tall bracket signal
behind the footbridge controlled the
junction, and in spite of its greater
height the left-hand arm was for the
branch to Walton, and the right-
hand for the main line to Clacton.
This apparent anomaly is explained
by the layout of the junction, as it is
the main line that curves away to
the right, while the branch goes
straight on.
Real Photographs (K175)

Top right:
Walton-on-Naze seen in April 1949
with Class F6 2-4-2T No 7220 waiting
with a train. Note the sidings and
turntable: the branch is now
reduced to one-train working
beyond Kirby Cross, and this is the
only platform left at Walton.
Real Photographs (K174)

Right:
Class B1 No 61329 arriving at
Clacton on 21 May 1957 with the
4.50pm stopping train from
Colchester. Within a month, work to
electrify the branch was under way.
John Brodribb collection

Below right:
Class N7 No 69620 works a stopping
train into Walton in May 1957, again
just before the start of
electrification. This locomotive was
one of the many of its class
displaced from the London area
suburban services by electric trains.
John Brodribb collection

25

eft:
*entley Junction again, this time with Class B1 No 61055 in
charge of the Norwich to London milk train one day in 1950.
The six-wheeled flat wagons conveying road tankers are of
particular note; the remainder was carried in churns in the
other vehicles. This traffic has now gone completely from
he railways.* A. R. J. Frost

ottom left:
*Not far from Bentley and the main line in distance – just
ver two miles – but worlds away in the general pace of
ailway life. Class J17 No 65512 heads the Hadleigh branch*

freight at Capel St Mary on 21 April 1958. The deserted
country road is the A12! *John Brodribb collection*

Below:
On 6 June 1959 4-6-2 No 70005 *John Milton* is about to enter
Ipswich tunnel at the head of the 3.38pm London to
Yarmouth South Town train. Behind it is the site of the
original station, disused for passengers for over a century at
this time, and latterly the home of the Ipswich motive
power depot. The River Orwell is also in view, with a Fisons
depot on the far bank at Cliff Quay, served by a freight-only
branch. *A. R. J. Frost*

Above:
Ipswich, seen from the other end of the tunnel. When first built, only one platform was provided, and the up 'East Anglian' is seen leaving from it; it is now called Platform 2. The island platform, with faces numbered 3 and 4, was added later; the carriage sidings are on the left of this. Two locomotives wait their turn of duty in the foreground; these short sidings were used when up trains had to change locomotives. Rows of wagons can just be seen in the Lower Yard, behind the bus. *G. R. Mortimer*

Below:
Class E4 2-4-0 No 62797 waits in the drizzle at the front of Platform 3 at Ipswich with the 8.50am to Cambridge on 24 July 1957. Locomotives of this class were the last 2-4-0 tender engines to work on British Railways. Note the tender cab. *John Brodribb collection*

A scene familiar to many East Anglian enthusiasts: Class B1 No 61054 is seen from Platform 4 marshalling stock in the carriage sidings at Ipswich on 18 July 1958.
John Brodribb collection

Below:
The 'Mail' was always an important train; No 70008 *Black Prince* leaves Ipswich with the 6.45pm from Norwich on 23 May 1958. The fine ex-LNER vehicle behind the locomotive is of especial interest.
John Brodribb collection

Above:
Fisons was an important employer in the area for many years, and many gardeners will be familiar with the name of Levington, a small village on the Orwell estuary. Class B1 No 61160 heads a chartered special to Windsor, due out at 10.05am on 31 May 1958. *John Brodribb collection*

Right:
North of Ipswich station, Class J17 No 65524 has just passed East Suffolk Junction, and takes the Norwich line with a Class F freight on 10 October 1951. The cattle truck behind the engine conveyed another traffic that no longer goes by rail. *R. E. Vincent*

Top right:
A clean 'Britannia' class engine, No 70011 *Hotspur* of Norwich shed, works the 9.55am stopping train from Norwich Thorpe to Ipswich, seen here shortly after leaving Bramford on 3 August 1953. *A. R. Carpenter*

Bottom right:
A busy scene at Stowmarket as No 70036 *Boadicea* runs in with the up 'Broadsman' on 17 September 1958. On the down platform milk churns and pigeon crates are evidence of other traffic. Stowmarket station has recently been modernised in connection with electrification, but very much in sympathy with the style shown here, being a listed building. *John Brodribb collection*

Above:
**Class D16/3 No 62521 leaves Stowmarket on the 2.00pm
Cambridge to Ipswich train on a day in July 1956; note the
van conveyed as tail traffic. Class J67 No 68518 was the
Stowmarket shunter, and was replaced by a diesel
locomotive shortly afterwards.** *Dr Ian C. Allen*

Below:
**Haughley Junction – just read that nameboard! Class D16/3
4-4-0 No 62566 and Class B17 4-6-0 No 61645 *The Suffolk
Regiment* run in on a Cambridge to Ipswich working. The
Mid-Suffolk train can just be glimpsed behind the leading
engine.** *Real Photographs (K188)*

Top right:
**Haughley Junction bustles with activity on 23 July 1952.
The 10.22am Ipswich to Bury St Edmunds stands in the
down main platform, while a 'J15' has the road for Laxfield.
The station had recently been modified to incorporate a bay**

platform for the Mid-Suffolk trains – previously they had
had their own station. The service was withdrawn shortly
afterwards! *R. E. Vincent*

Centre right:
**Class J15 No 5459 is seen standing at Kenton in April 1949.
This was the only passing place on the Mid-Suffolk, and the
site for the only fixed signalling. Some fairly involved
shunting took place here, which can't have helped the
average speeds of mixed trains. Nationalisation seems to
have passed by Kenton completely.**
Real Photographs (K187)

Bottom right:
**The terminus of the Mid-Suffolk line at Laxfield. Apart from
Kenton, facilities here were as extensive as anywhere on
the line. It had once extended as far as Cratfield, about 2¼
miles further on, but never reached its goal of Halesworth.
Class J15 No 5459 waits with a train for Haughley in April
1949.** *Real Photographs (K185)*

Above:
The old and the new at Mellis Junction in June 1956. Class J17 No 65542 stands with the Eye branch goods, while a new and shiny diesel multiple unit leaves on a Norwich to Ipswich train. *Dr Ian C. Allen*

Below:
Tivetshall was the junction for the Waveney Valley line to Beccles. A source of traffic can be seen in the extensive maltings in the background; meanwhile Class E4 No 62787 waits to leave on the branch train to, as the sign says, 'the Pulhams, Harleston, Bungay and Beccles'. *Real Photographs (K182)*

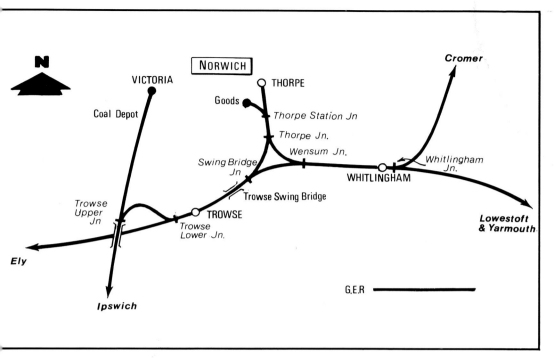

N

VICTORIA

Coal Depot

Norwich

Goods

THORPE

Thorpe Station Jn

Thorpe Jn.

Wensum Jn.

Cromer

Swing Bridge
Jn

Whitlingham
Jn.

WHITLINGHAM

Trowse Swing Bridge

Trowse
Upper
Jn

TROWSE

Trowse
Lower Jn.

Lowestoft
& Yarmouth

Ely

Ipswich

G.E.R ━━━━━━━

Below:
Traffic from the Cambridge and Ipswich lines into Norwich has to cross the River Wensum by the swing bridge at Trowse. The first bridge on the site was built in 1846 for the opening of the line from Brandon into Norwich, and was single-track. It was rebuilt in 1906 as a double-track electrically-operated structure, and the speed limit raised to 15mph. It is proposed to rebuild it again in connection with the electrification of the line from London, in which case the overhead wires will have to move with the bridge. In this photograph, Class D16/3 No 62523 heads the 4.25pm Norwich to Dereham train on 11 September 1954.
R. E. Vincent

Top:
A typically stirring departure from Norwich Thorpe is made by No 7001? *Oliver Cromwell* **on the up 'East Anglian' on an April day in 1961.**
J. S. Whiteley

Above:
The same train, distinguished by a headboard on this occasion, stands at Platform 4 on the point of departure on 1 March 1958. 'Britannia' class No 70002 *Geoffrey Chaucer* **has steam to spare for the two-hour journey to London.**
John Brodribb collection

Left:
By contrast, Class B12 No 61547 stands at the same platform, No 4, with a train headed in the opposite direction: the 12.30pm from Liverpool Street to Sheringham, also on 1 March 1958. The train had arrived at Norwich behind Class B1 No 61005 *Bongo*.
John Brodribb collection

Above:
The other side of Norwich Thorpe is seen on 29 August 1950, as Class J20 No 4696 leaves with the 2.29pm Class F freight to Goodmayes. The J20s were originally introduced in 1920, and were rebuilt from 1943 onwards with the same boilers as the Class B12/3 4-6-0s; they had a considerably higher tractive effort than the latter. *E. Tuddenham*

Below:
The East Suffolk line to Yarmouth and Lowestoft diverges from the Norwich line at East Suffolk Junction, just north of Ipswich, and describes an arc so that at Westerfield Junction trains were heading almost due east. In this wintry 1956 view from the signalbox at Westerfield, Class L1 No 67706 heads a Felixstowe train; the fireman prepares to take the tablet for the single line to Derby Road. When the branch to Felixstowe opened, trains terminated in the bay platform shown here; the original station building is on the extreme left. *A. R. J. Frost*

Above:

Above:

Felixstowe Town sidings on 26 August 1959, with Shunter Jennings poised for action. A skilled shunter made the job look easy, but in reality it could be hard and potentially dangerous work, especially on a cold wet night. Note that the coupling on the wagon here is well-greased for easy action. *A. R. J. Frost*

Below:
Another scene at Felixstowe, showing Class L1 2-6-4T No 67775 in action. These powerful engines were a familiar sight on the branch; they were designed by Edward Thompson and first introduced in 1945. *A. R. J. Frost*

Above:
A view of Felixstowe Town station in the 1960s, which shows the extensive layout: four platforms each capable of holding a 15-coach excursion train; goods shed and yards; extensive awnings; and a large station building with ample facilities. All that now remains is one track, which terminates about halfway along the train of flat wagons; the rest is a supermarket and car-park.
R. Whipps collection

Below:
Felixstowe Beach station in the 1960s. This line is very much in use today for container traffic to and from the docks, but passenger services were finally withdrawn on 11 September 1967. *R. Whipps collection*

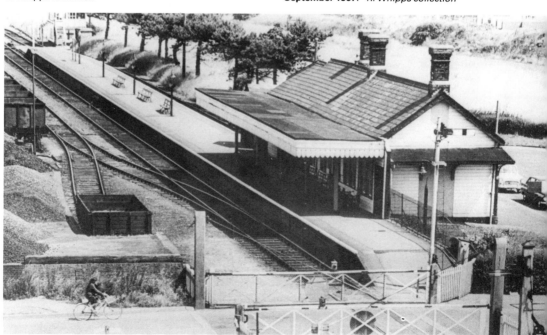

A scene which persisted to the end of the 1950s in many places was shunting by means of horses. This fine view taken at Woodbridge shows a double-headed movement through the down platform, while the stationmaster supervises.
Suffolk Photographic Survey, County Hall, Ipswich

Below:
Wickham Market (the station is really in Campsea Ashe) was the starting point for Framlingham branch trains. There was no bay platform, so the branch train had to wait in a siding until the down platform was clear. In April 1949 Class F3 2-4-2T No 7150 is in charge. *Real Photographs (K181)*

Above:
The junction for Framlingham was about a mile down the line at Wickham Market Junction. Freight services outlasted passenger by about 12 years, finishing officially on 19 April 1965. Class J15 No 65389 is hardly overtaxed as it comes off the branch with the daily working in 1959.
John Brodribb collection

Centre:
With only a few weeks to go before withdrawal, Class F6 2-4-2T No 67230 heads the 1.40pm Wickham Market to Framlingham train shortly after leaving Parham. The splendid Great Eastern distant signals, with arms for both directions on opposite sides of the one post, are of great interest. *G. H. Mortimer*

Below:
Apologies may be due for this photograph of a diesel shunter at Snape: however, it is very much a steam-age scene. The Fordson tractor is working a wagon across the road, protected by a flagman: British Railways locomotives were not permitted to cross the road into the maltings. The poster on the fence announces the withdrawal of freight services from Snape, Aldeburgh and Thorpeness; the date is 16 April 1959. *John Brodribb collection*

Left:
Looking the other way, two wagons are shunted through the archway, much more familiar today to music lovers as the entrance to Snape Maltings concert hall, where a large part of the annual Aldeburgh festival is held. There was an extensive system of sidings which served the maltings of Messrs Swonnells, and also a wharf where traffic was exchanged between railway and barge. In the days before tractors were used, shunting was by horses.
John Brodribb collection

Below:
Steam power at Saxmundham on 21 August 1958. There were two level crossings at the station, one of which bisected the down platform and necessitated the use of a movable platform section instead of a gate. The other, shown here, separated the up and down platforms. Class B12 No 61535 restarts the 8.33am from Liverpool Street to Yarmouth South Town, while Class B17/6 No 61618 *Wynard Park* stands at the up platform with the 9.53am Yarmouth South Town to Liverpool Street.
John Brodribb collection

Above:
**Aldeburgh branch trains started from Saxmundham and in
this view Class J15 No 65467 is seen between the station
and Saxmundham Junction with the 5.52pm on 5 April
1956. The gradient on the main line is considerable at this
point, and after slowing for the crossover to take the
branch, Aldeburgh trains faced an even steeper climb for a
further half-mile or so.** *Philip J. Kelley*

Below:
**A scene typical of many former Great Eastern branches:
Class J17 No 65560 heads the Aldeburgh goods back to
Ipswich, here seen between Thorpeness and Leiston in
September 1956. This was a conditional working, booked
out of Ipswich at 7.10am and calling at all stations as
required.** *Dr Ian C. Allen*

Bottom:
Class J15 No 65467 simmers quietly 'on shed' at Aldeburgh on 13 July 1955. Diesel units arrived on passenger services the following year, and for a time offered through running to Ipswich and even Colchester. However, the service was withdrawn on 12 September 1966, and the line closed completely between Aldeburgh and Sizewell siding.
Eric A. Brookes

Below:
Another of the ubiquitous J15s, this time No 65447 standing at Aldeburgh in April 1956 ready to return to Saxmundham.
Real Photographs (K2862)

Right:
Great activity at Beccles, the major junction on the East Suffolk line. Class B17 No 61669 *Barnsley* waits at the up main platform with a Yarmouth to Liverpool Street express, while auto-fitted Class F5 2-4-2T No 67199 is in the down main platform, probably on a stopping train to Yarmouth. The curved structure seen at rail level is part of a movable platform bridge, which can be seen swung back into the up platform beside No 61669. It allowed heavy items such as churns to be moved easily and safely across the track, but was operationally awkward because it had to be fully-interlocked with the signalling.
Real Photographs (K2276)

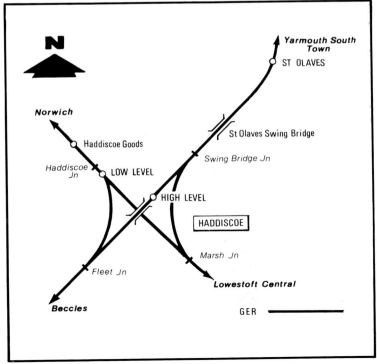

Left:
At the other end of Beccles station activity is also intense as Class E4 No 62789 leaves with the 3.25pm Waveney Valley train to Tivetshall, at the same time as Class J17 No 65559 departs with a Lowestoft working. Part of the extensive cattle docks can be seen. The date is 6 September 1952. *R. E. Vincent*

Above:
The lines to Yarmouth and Lowestoft diverged at Beccles North Junction; the signalbox there also controlled access to the Waveney Valley line. A Class J15 takes the Lowestoft portion of the 'Easterling' on the final stage of its journey, the six Yarmouth coaches having left several minutes earlier. The motive power of the two parts provided quite a contrast – the main train would have had a 'Britannia' class Pacific! *R. E. Vincent*

Above:
Northwards from Beccles, the East Suffolk crossed the Lowestoft to Norwich line at Haddiscoe, where there were high and low-level platforms. The 1.01pm from Yarmouth South Town to Beccles has just left the high level station, headed by Class F5 No 67199, on 21 April 1954. This part of Haddiscoe station was reconstructed by the LNER in a rather severe-looking concrete style in 1936; the date is cast into the abutments of the now-demolished bridge.
R. E. Vincent

Below:
The 12.26pm Lowestoft to Norwich train pulls away from Haddiscoe low level on 20 April 1954. The station was noted for its immaculate appearance and the gardens are obviously well-tended. Haddiscoe Junction signalbox is clearly visible; it is now in the Science Museum at South Kensington. *R. E. Vincent*

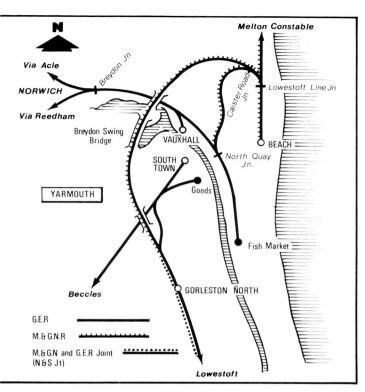

N

Melton Constable

Via Acle

NORWICH

Via Reedham

Breydon Jn

Breydon Swing
Bridge

VAUXHALL

Caister Road Jn

Lowestoft Line Jn

BEACH

North Quay
Jn.

SOUTH
TOWN

Goods

YARMOUTH

Fish Market

Beccles

GORLESTON NORTH

G.E.R

M.&G.N.R

M.&G.N and G.E.R Joint
(N&S Jt)

Lowestoft

Below:

**Yarmouth South Town handled almost
all the express trains to London, as
well as local services to Beccles and
Lowestoft. It was extensively rebuilt
in 1953, work which was somewhat
disrupted by the severe flooding of
that year. Class B17 No 61622
Alnwick Castle waits to leave with a
Liverpool Street train in 1958.**
John Brodribb collection

Above:
Class F5 2-4-2T No 67199 waits at South Town with a train for Beccles in June 1954. The running time allowed was 26 minutes for the 12½ miles, with four intermediate stops. Some of these local trains were extended to or from Saxmundham.
Real Photographs (K2277)

Below:
Taking one of the other routes out of Beccles, the Waveney Valley goods approaches Lowestoft Central, headed by Class J15 No 65462. *H. N. James*

Right:
On a sunny June day in 1954 Class F5 No 67218 stands in Platform 1 at Lowestoft Central on a push-pull working to Yarmouth South Town via Gorleston – the 'New Line'. Lowestoft Central was – and is – Britain's most easterly railway station, and lives up to its name, being very conveniently sited. Until 1953, when Breydon Bridge was closed, several of the local trains to Yarmouth worked into Beach station; Lowestoft also received through trains this way from the Midlands via the Midland & Great Northern line.
Real Photographs (K2274)

Below right:
Being an East Coast port with a fine harbour, Lowestoft had an extensive network of dockside lines on both sides of Lake Lothing. Lowestoft South Side and Kirkley were served by the branch from Oulton Broad South, which had several private sidings such as those of the Co-op, and Boulton & Paul. The fish quay, on the other side, was reached by a line which crossed the main A12 just outside Central station, and contributed considerably to traffic congestion, although the lifting bridge which took the road over Lake Lothing also played its part – and still does. The Great Eastern, and later the London & North Eastern, Railways used Lowestoft for the import of timber, and established a large sleeper depot there. Various classes of small, short wheelbase shunters were used over the years, such as the Class Y3 0-4-0T No 40 (formerly No 68173) shown here. They were geared locomotives, made by Sentinel.
H. N. James

Above:

Yarmouth and Lowestoft have long been rivals as ports and resorts. Yarmouth certainly had more railway termini; Vauxhall was the Great Eastern station for the Midlands and North. It was rebuilt in the 1950s, and Class J19/2 No 64643 is seen bringing empty stock into Platform 2 in August 1960. *John C. Baker*

Below:

There was an extensive system of street and quay lines in Yarmouth necessitating the use of tram-type locomotives, with enclosed motion and wheels. One of the more unusual was 'Y10' No 68186, the sole member of its class, seen here in Vauxhall Yard. *E. M. Patterson*

It was possible to reach Norwich from Yarmouth by two routes, via Acle or via Reedham. The two converge at Brundall, where Class D16/3 No 62586 is seen in September 1956 on the 11.50am Saturdays-only train from Norwich to Yarmouth via Reedham. *Dr Ian C. Allen*

Swing bridges are a feature of East Anglian railways, being necessitated by the combination of flat terrain and navigable waterways. They are now electrically-driven, and have to be fitted with ingenious means of allowing the signal wires and point rodding to engage and disengage as the bridge is swung. It is ironic that two of the most modern, which had the least limitations of speed, were among the first to be demolished when the East Suffolk line north of Beccles was closed: the bridges were at Beccles and St Olaves. In this unusual view, Somerleyton Swing Bridge, on the Lowestoft to Norwich line, is open for river traffic. *A. T. Jarvis*

Above:
Bungay, on the Waveney Valley line, seen on 1 September 1951. Class F5 No 67186 waits in the platform, while Class E4 No 62789 runs in with the photographer's train. This station site is now completely obliterated by the Bungay by-pass, although other stations are relatively well-preserved. *H. C. Casserley*

Left:
The Great Eastern ran to Sheringham, on the Midland & Great Northern Joint line, and although the LNER took over the M&GN completely in 1936, this sign was still in place in 1958. *John Brodribb collection*

Right:
Until closure in 1954, Great Eastern line trains from Norwich ran into Cromer High, and then reversed back to Cromer Junction, and reversed again, this time going towards Roughton Road Junction to gain access to the M&GN. After 1954 they ran via Roughton Road, Newstead Lane and Runton East Junctions to reach the much-more convenient Cromer Beach, there reversing to go to Sheringham. On 3rd March 1958 Ivatt Class 4MT No 43155 waits in the yard at Cromer Beach with a short freight.
John Brodribb collection

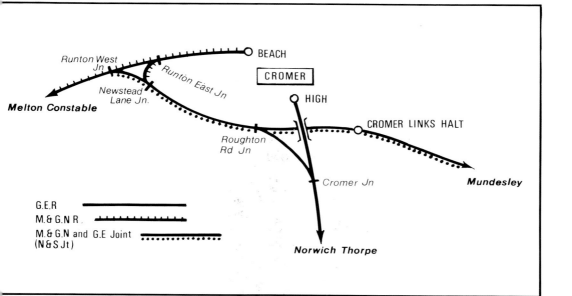

G.E.R   ————————
M.&G.N.R   ++++++++++
M.&G.N and G.E Joint   ••••••••••••
(N&S Jt)

Top:
As an important junction and traffic centre, Dereham had its own locomotive shed (a sub-shed to Norwich) where Class J17 No 65516 is seen in September 1953. A Class J15 0-6-0 is under cover. *Real Photographs (K2041)*

Above:
Class J17 No 65567 has just taken water at Dereham, whilst heading an RCTS special train in March 1962.
Real Photographs (K4922)

Top right:
On the Wells line, Class J15 No 65471 climbs towards Dereham with the afternoon milk train from North Elmham to Norwich Thorpe in May 1960. *M. J. Esau*

Centre right:
Further again towards the North Norfolk coast, Class D16/3 No 62577 heads the 3.45pm Sundays only from Wells to Norwich near Ryburgh on 24 July 1955. *E. Tuddenham*

Bottom right:
Reepham station, between County School and Aylsham, is seen with Class F6 No 67224 leaving at the head of the 2.33pm Wroxham to Dereham train on 12 September 1951. *E. Tuddenham*

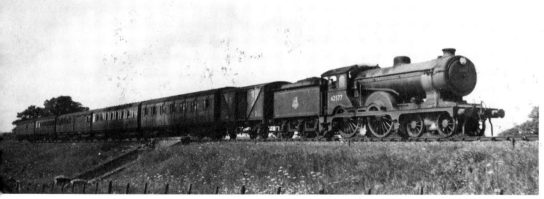

Below:

Class J17 No 65519 is engaged on track recovery in the Reepham to Foulsham section on 22 March 1957. This part of the line had been closed to all traffic on 15 September 1952, but following lifting, the track from Reepham to Thelmelthorpe was reinstated in 1960 after the M&GN had closed. This allowed freight trains to work to and from Norwich City without having to go all the way round via Melton Constable and Sheringham. *E. Tuddenham*

Bottom:

The lines from Marks Tey to Cambridge formed an important cross-country link for passengers and freight. Chappel & Wakes Colne is the first station on the line after Marks Tey. It became a junction in 1860 when the first part of the Colne Valley line opened as far as Halstead, the line to Sudbury having been open some 11 years at that time. The Colne Valley subsequently extended to Haverhill, where trains could rejoin the line from Sudbury. The Colne Valley Railway remained independent until the Grouping in 1923, and some trains left Marks Tey formed from both CVR and Great Eastern stock, then dividing at Chappel. This practice lasted into the early 1950s. The train shown here is the 11.04am Cambridge to Colchester via Sudbury, seen on 21 April 1958. The Great Eastern footbridge was demolished after the line to Sudbury was reduced to 'basic railway' status, but has since been replaced by the Stour Valley Preservation Society with one from Sudbury, which gives access to the society's depot in the former goods yard.
John Brodribb collection

Above:

...t out of Chappel, where Ivatt Class 2 2-6-0 No 46468
...ds the 4.30pm train from Marks Tey to Haverhill via the
...ne Valley line on 12 September 1957. The train has only
...t traversed the junction with the Stour Valley line.
...R. Mortimer.

...ht:

...original Colne Valley Railway cast-iron notice at
...appel, which had survived the transitions to LNER and BR
...nership: it was photographed on 21 April 1958.
...n Brodribb collection

MOTOR CAR ACTS 1896 AND 1903

NOTICE.

THIS BRIDGE IS INSUFFICIENT TO CARRY A HEAVY
MOTOR CAR THE REGISTERED AXLE WEIGHT OF ANY
AXLE OF WHICH EXCEEDS THREE TONS, OR THE
REGISTERED AXLE WEIGHTS OF THE SEVERAL AXLES
OF WHICH EXCEED IN THE AGGREGATE FIVE TONS OR A
HEAVY MOTOR CAR DRAWING A TRAILER, IF THE
REGISTERED AXLE WEIGHTS OF THE SEVERAL AXLES
OF THE HEAVY MOTOR CAR AND THE AXLE WEIGHTS
OF THE SEVERAL AXLES OF THE TRAILER EXCEED IN
THE AGGREGATE FIVE TONS.

COLNE VALLEY RAILWAY COMPANY.
...T C HAW...
SECRETARY. HALSTEAD, E...

the Stour Valley line, trains leaving Chappel travelled via
es and Sudbury to Long Melford. Here the branch to
y St Edmunds continued in a northerly direction, while
Cambridge line swung westwards. This fine view of the
ion and junction shows Class B2 No 61639 arriving from
nbridge on a Colchester train in April 1956.
I Photographs (K2865)

ow left:
rural railway is epitomised by the Class J15 taking
er at Long Melford whilst working the 11.52am Marks
to Cambridge train on 27 March 1954. *R. E. Vincent*

Below:
The local branch line was an unchanging and permanent
part of the countryside: it was something that had always
been there as long as almost anyone could remember. Here
Glemsford signalbox is seen in the summer of 1966; the line
closed in March 1967. *P. Hocquard*

Cavendish was the next station along the line from Glemsford, where the signalman is seen in action near to the closure. The layout at the station has already been simplified: there are several white levers in the frame, **although the handles are still brightly burnished. In fact, the line closed for freight about six months before withdrawal of passenger services. Note here the single-line tablet instrument, and the oil-lamp overhead.** *P. Hocquard*

Below:
The charm of rural Suffolk: Class J15 No 65446 takes water at Haverhill on 14 April 1959, while the engine crew enjoys a yarn. *John Brodribb collection*

Bottom:
Haverhill station, looking towards Cambridge. It was known for a while as Haverhill North, since the Colne Valley had its own station called Haverhill South. Even before the Grouping, CVR trains often used the North station, so that onward connections could be made to Cambridge, and after take-over by the LNER South was relegated to goods-only status and eventually closed. *Real Photographs (K163)*

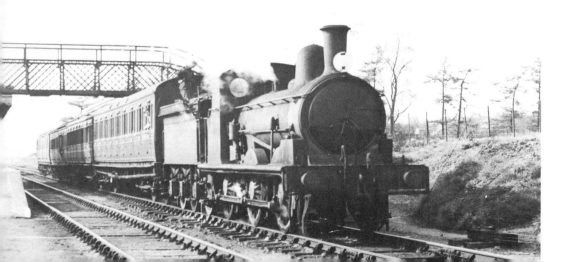

Above:
Six miles towards Cambridge was Bartlow, junction for the Saffron Walden branch. Class J17 No 65575 passes through with a Cambridge to Marks Tey freight on 16 April 1949.
W. A. Camwell

Left:
The branch platform at Bartlow in February 1958, where a Class N7 is arriving with a train from Saffron Walden. Latterly this service was worked by these engines after their displacement from the London area, with pairs of auto-coaches. This looks like the mid-afternoon train, loaded with schoolchildren. *A. J. Willmott*

Top right:
A Class J15 locomotive heads the 11.04am from Cambridge to Colchester near Shelford on 28 August 1957. The identity of the engine seems a little doubtful: it carries the number 65291 on the smokebox, and 65391 on the cabside!
J. A. Coiley

Bottom right:
Bury St Edmunds was the major station on the cross-country line from Ipswich to Cambridge and Ely. Additionally, branches from Thetford and Long Melford converged here; in this photograph a Class F6 2-4-2T heads the 10.40am for Thetford on 25 April 1953. Passenger services were withdrawn in June of that year, but freight survived until 1960. *G. R. Mortimer*

Above:
One of the twin towers of Bury St Edmunds station stands watch over No 46465, which has arrived from Sudbury with a pick-up freight in May 1961. *John C. Baker*

Below:
This study of the station at Cockfield, on the Bury St Edmunds to Long Melford line, has a wealth of detail. All the signals are interesting: the tall lattice post bearing arms for both directions, and the old-pattern ground signal between the board crossings. Note the oil lamps in their housings, and the elderly, much-patched van body acting as a store. The picture was taken from the rear coach of a train in August 1957. *A. J. Willmott*

The lines from Bury to Cambridge and Ely diverged at Chippenham Junction, and a short distance along the former was Newmarket old station and Warren Hill tunnel, the longest in East Anglia, single-track and an operational bottleneck. The old station, shown here, was used for horse traffic, as is evident from the vans. Class J17 No 65532 has just emerged from the tunnel with an eastbound freight on 22 May 1958. *G. R. Mortimer*

Class J15 No 65468 pilots Class D16/3 No 62610 out of Cambridge on the 2.00pm stopping train to Newmarket and Ipswich on 22 May 1957. The reason for the excess motive power is not clear, although the J15 seems to be doing all the work. The D16 is carrying a headcode disc – is it perhaps a failure? *J. A. Coiley*

Top left:
The closure of the Thetford to Bury line is only a fortnight away as Class J17 No 65589 passes Ingham on a goods train from Thetford on 10 June 1960. The days when rabbit skins were an important traffic have long since gone.
H. N. James

Bottom left:
Thetford station itself, with a local train from Bury having just arrived; the date is April 1949, and the locomotive Class F6 No 7236. *Real Photographs (K189)*

Above:
Apart from the main line, the other route away from Thetford was that to Swaffham. This Class D16/3 is working a train from Swaffham to Thetford at Watton on 12 October 1951. The rail-built gas lamp is worthy of note.
G. J. Jefferson

Right:
Services through Swaffham had been dieselised for some years when this picture was taken shortly before closure on 7 September 1968. This gap lamp was typical of the area, and very much a part of the steam era. *John A. M. Vaughan*

SWAFFHAM

Top left:
Moving over now to the main line from Liverpool Street to Cambridge, Elsenham station sees the 2.28pm for Thaxted waiting in the branch platform. Meanwhile, a Whitemoor to Temple Mills freight passes on the main line, headed by Class K1 No 62070. *R. E. Vincent*

Bottom left:
In complete contrast Class B17 No 61620 *Clumber* is seen on the main line near Elsenham with the 1.10pm Fridays and Saturdays-only train from Cambridge to Liverpool Street on 29 August 1952. *R. E. Vincent*

Above:
Some six years later at Audley End tunnel, where 'Britannia' class No 70009 *Alfred the Great* heads the 1.32pm Norwich to Liverpool Street via Cambridge on 21 May 1958. There were still several Norwich to London workings via this route at this time, although they tended to stop at most stations between Norwich and Cambridge, and the service via Ipswich offered faster overall journeys. *G. R. Mortimer*

Right:
Saffron Walden suffered by not being on the main line, and had to be content with a shuttle service to Audley End. Some trains ran through to Bartlow, such as this working with an ex-Great Northern Class C12 4-4-2T in May 1947. *A. J. Willmott*

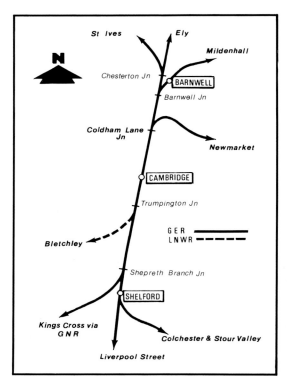

St Ives
Ely
Mildenhall
Chesterton Jn
BARNWELL
Barnwell Jn
Coldham Lane Jn
Newmarket
CAMBRIDGE
Trumpington Jn
G E R ——————
L N W R ----------
Bletchley
Shepreth Branch Jn
SHELFORD
Kings Cross via GNR
Colchester & Stour Valley
Liverpool Street

Below:
And so to Cambridge, for a look around the station. Being a major junction, there was a variety of trains; in pre-Grouping days the Great Eastern, Great Northern, London & North Western and Midland all worked regularly into Cambridge, and some of this variety lasted well into the era of nationalisation. In this photograph, the celebrated No 70000 *Britannia*, of Stratford shed, waits to leave for Ely and Norwich on 6 July 1957. *John Brodribb collection*

Right:
In complete contrast, Class J15 No 65438 arrives with the Saturdays-only 11.49am from Mildenhall on the same date. The ground signals are of very great age and, to modern eyes, very antiquated.
John Brodribb collection

74

Top:
An unusual visitor to Cambridge restarts the 4.35pm
Sundays-only Kings Cross to York train, passing the
magnificent signal gantry. Class A1 Pacific No 60138
Boswell had stopped to set down passengers for a
connecting bus service to Huntingdon on 8 May 1960, the
Great Northern main line being closed for engineering
work. *G. D. King*

Above:
A very short distance out of Cambridge sees Standard Class
5MT No 73071 making fine progress with the 11.08am
Buffet Express to Kings Cross on 11 January 1957. *J. A.
Coiley*

Above:
In the opposite direction, Class J39 No 64772 pulls past Cambridge North signalbox with the 1.05pm trip from Tenison Fields Yard to Whitemoor with coal empties on 10 June 1961. *G. D. King*

Below:
More freight traffic as Ivatt Class 2 No 46467 leaves Trumpington goods loop, just to the south of Cambridge, with the daily Class K freight for Clare on 7 July 1961. The sidings in the background are mostly full of conflats awaiting the end of the Royal Show. *M. J. Fox*

Far left:
Just north of Cambridge the main line crosses the River Cam, and beyond the bridge is Chesterton Junction, the signalbox just visible in this picture. Class J15 No 65478 has just come off the St Ives line with a local freight for Cambridge on 18 April 1961. *G. D. King*

Bottom left:
The first station on the line to St Ives was Histon, where on a fine June day No 70034 *Thomas Hardy* leaves on the 2.57pm Cambridge to March parcels train. *M. Barratt*

Left: Below:
The Mildenhall branch left the main line at Barnwell Junction, and took a gentle course across the edge of the Fens. One of the intermediate stations was at Burwell, which was provided with a passing loop, and a capacious station building for the sparse service. These two photographs show Class E4 No 62796, fitted with a tender cab, about to pull under the bridge with a Mildenhall train, and returning later, bound for Cambridge. Both photographs date from 1957: the branch was dieselised in the following year. *A. J. Willmott*

Right:
Class E4 No 62796 again features on a Mildenhall train, but this time at Fordham on the Bury St Edmunds to Ely line, where the Mildenhall branch crossed the main line. The passenger who has just alighted doesn't seem to be crossing the track by the footbridge only, but is probably hoping to get through the level crossing gates, which are just being swung open. *A. J. Willmott*

Below:
Journey's end on this particular branch: the terminus at Mildenhall has Class J15 No 65438 waiting with a Cambridge train on 30 November 1957. *L. King*

Far right:
Another cross-country branch went from St Ives to Ely. Here Class J15 No 65457 works an excursion from Bluntisham to Hunstanton via Ely, pulling into Earith Bridge at 10.16am on 1 August 1955. The overgrown appearance is partly accounted for by the fact that regular passenger services had been withdrawn on 2 February 1931. *T. B. Paisley*

Below right:
In contrast, two freight trains pass at Haddenham on the same line. The locomotives are WD 2-8-0 No 90630 and Standard Class 4MT No 75003. The line closed as a through route in 1958, although Haddenham remained open until 1964. *M. J. Esau*

Above:
Chesterton Junction again, with the St Ives line curving away behind the locomoive, No 70011 *Hotspur*. **It is in charge of the 8.20am Liverpool Street to Norwich train on Sunday 29 May 1960.** *G. D. King*

Below:
Ely was an important junction, although entirely on former Great Eastern territory, unlike Cambridge. On 4 March 1961 Ivatt Class 2 No 46465 has worked the 8.50am stopping train from Cambridge via Newmarket, the usual diesel multiple-unit presumably having failed. *M. J. Fox*

Above:
The former status of March as a railway centre is obvious when seen on a map, although much less so today. Whitemoor Yard handled huge tonnages of freight, mainly coal, much of which arrived on the Great Northern & Great Eastern Joint line via Spalding. In April 1961 Class J20 No 64690 heads a train of coal empties through the station, bound for Whitemoor. *John C. Baker*

Below:
Looking the other way at March, along the main line towards Peterborough, whence 'Black Five' No 45111 has come with a train from Birmingham. It is just leaving for Clacton, and is thought to have worked the train as far as Colchester. *G. D. King*

Top left:
Wisbech had most railway facilities duplicated by the M&GN and Great Eastern lines; both had harbour branches, but on opposite sides of the River Nene. In March 1953 Class J15 No 65422 leaves the GER line with a freight for March.
P. J. Lynch

Far left:
23 March 1953 sees the then-oldest Class J15, No 65356, shunting Wisbech goods yard. The significance of the smokebox adornments isn't immediately obvious. *P. J. Lynch*

Above:
No mention of Wisbech would be complete without the locomotives which worked the tramway to Upwell. The passenger service was withdrawn on 2 January 1928, but freight lasted until 1966. Until 1952 it was handled by locomotives such as No 68222, of Class J70, seen in June of that year. *P. Ransome-Wallis*

Left:
A rather more conventional view of Wisbech East, as the Great Eastern station was latterly known, sees Class D16/3 No 62618 on a Kings Lynn to March train on 27 July 1952. The rolling stock is certainly varied, even to the extent of the second coach being of the clerestory type.
P. H. Wells

Above:

King's Lynn is a port on the Wash, and this generated considerable traffic locally, although a substantial amount continued inland via the waterways. As a railway centre it was very important, and because the station is a terminus, many trains had to reverse there. On 15 February 1958 Ivatt Class 4 No 43095 waits at the far platform with the 11.50am to Yarmouth Beach via the M&GN, while Class B17 No 61621 *Hatfield House* heads the 11.55am to Wisbech and March. *E. Wilmshurst*

Below:

King's Lynn again, with Class B17 No 61635 *Milton* leaving with a local working on 29 October 1956. Class D16/3 No 62545 lurks behind. *L. G. Marshall*

A fine study of Class J69 No 68499 at King's Lynn during a break in shunting. Note that the engine retains the encased 'Ramsbottom' pattern of safety valves; the earlier style of 'British Railways' lettering is clearly visible underneath the newer crest. *L. G. Marshall*

A variety of locomotives is seen on shed at King's Lynn in October 1953, including three 'Claud Hamiltons' – the much-rebuilt Class D16/3s. The leading one is No 62579. *B. K. B. Green*

Left:

Wolferton, on the Hunstanton branch, was used for Royal Trains almost as soon as the then-Prince of Wales, later King Edward VII, acquired the Sandringham estate in 1862. Traffic was such that the line from King's Lynn to Wolferton was doubled in 1898, and the station was rebuilt in regal style. Even the station lamps had their adornments – compare the picture of Wolferton with the lamp at Swaffham. Today the station houses a museum which recalls the days of Royal Railways, and is well worth a visit. *P. Hocquard*

Below:

And so to the Midland & Great Northern Joint Railway. Formed by the amalgamation of a number of small lines, the M&GN first became an entity in the form of the Eastern & Midlands Railway, whose longest-lasting memorial seems to have been its roof brackets, seen here at Yarmouth Beach. Today they survive at Cromer Beach, though probably not for long. Yarmouth was the major destination for M&GN passengers, although connections were provided at Melton Constable for Norwich and Cromer, and some trains continued from Yarmouth to Gorleston and Lowestoft. *R. E. G. Read*

Below right:

Yarmouth Beach was one of the termini in that town used by the Norfolk & Suffolk Joint line from Lowestoft, the other being South Town. The other line built under the auspices of the N&S Jt was from North Walsham (strictly speaking, from Antingham Road Junction) to Runton West Junction, near Cromer. The line was intended to open up the northeast Norfolk coast to the holiday trade, and failed almost completely; but it left lavish railway facilities. This view of Mundesley gives a slight impression of its size. *Real Photographs (K2858)*

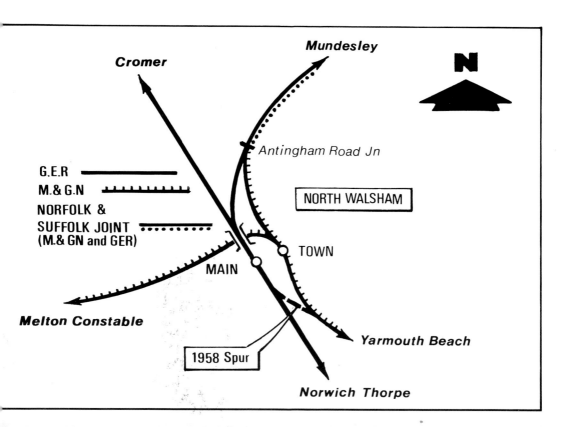

Cromer

Mundesley

N

G.E.R
M.&G.N
NORFOLK &
SUFFOLK JOINT
(M.& GN and GER)

Antingham Road Jn

NORTH WALSHAM

TOWN

MAIN

Melton Constable

1958 Spur

Yarmouth Beach

Norwich Thorpe

Above:
The line from Mundesley to Cromer closed on 17 April 1953, having had many economies imposed earlier. These are much in evidence at Overstrand on 6 April 1953, especially the lifted loop line on the other side of the island platform. Class F6 leaves with the 12.05pm Cromer Beach to North Walsham. *E. Tuddenham*

Left:
Between Potter Heigham and Yarmouth there were five halts, built to tap as much as possible of the seaside and Broadland holiday traffic and used only in the summer months. They were (from Potter Heigham) Potter Heigham Bridge Halt, Scratby, California, Caister Camp and Newtown Halts, the latter in Yarmouth. There were also four intermediate stations as well – Martham for Rollesby, Hemsby, Great Ormesby and Caister-on-Sea – and all of them in just under 13 miles! This photograph shows the rather basic nature of Potter Heigham Bridge Halt in summer 1949. *Photographer unknown*

Above: Below:
The main line westwards from Yarmouth went via Corpusty and Saxthorpe station. These views show ex-LMS 4F No 43937 pressed into passenger service on Whit Saturday 12 May 1951 near Corpusty, heading the 9.35am Birmingham New Street and Leicester London Road to Lowestoft via Bourne and Yarmouth Beach. The other shows the station on 8 August 1958, with Class J17 No 65551 running-in with a goods train for Melton Constable.
E. Tuddenham and Frank Church

Below:

All M&GN trains had to pass through Melton Constable, where the company had its headquarters and works. Connections were available there between the Cromer, Yarmouth and Norwich lines, and trains would be split or assembled there. Here Class D16/3 No 62578 is seen on shed. *Real Photographs (K2038)*

Bottom: Right:

Melton Constable in 1951, where a Class D16/3 is this time seen leaving with a Cromer train. In the other view, of Class 4 No 43148, a train is being re-formed by the attachment of a through coach from Derby. The locomotive is about to cross over to the far platform, by the bracket signals behind the bridge. The whole formation then left as the 2.31pm to Cromer Beach, the date being 30 August 1958. Trains from the Midlands could go straight through Melton for Norwich or Yarmouth, but had to reverse to go to Cromer.
N. Fields and G. R. Mortimer

Above:
Whitwell & Reepham looking towards Melton. Class J39 No 64968 stands with the 3.35pm Class J freight from Norwich City, while Class D16/3 enters the station with the 4.03pm from Melton Constable on 13 June 1957.
E. Tuddenham

Above:
Beyond Melton Constable, the M&GN main line went across country to South Lynn and Sutton Bridge where it divided, one line going to Spalding and Bourne, and the other to Wisbech and Peterborough. The first station out of Melton was Thursford, and Class 4MT No 43109 is seen near here with a Peterborough to Yarmouth Beach train on 22 September 1955. *Donald Kelk*

Below:
At the next town on the line, Fakenham, the M&GN crossed the Great Eastern line from Dereham to Wells. Fakenham thus had two stations, West and East, serving a town of about 3,500 population. Class 4MT No 43149 is seen heading a freight train towards Melton Constable through Fakenham West on 8 August 1958. *Frank Church*

Above:
The main line crossed the River Ouse just to the west of South Lynn by a single track bridge, which was inevitably an operating bottleneck. Here, Class 4MT No 43104 is coming off the bridge in June 1952 with a stopping train to Peterborough, and is about to regain the double track section. *P. Ransome-Wallis*

Below:
Looking west almost from the same spot in July 1952, Class 4MT No 43148 cautiously enters the single line section over the bridge with a train from the Midlands to Hunstanton. *P. Ransome-Wallis*

To end with, three pictures which show the heart of the steam railway. One locomotive class that epitomised the East Anglian branches was the elderly J15 0-6-0, capable of working the through portions of express trains, the pick-up goods, or whatever was asked. They were light enough to go almost anywhere. The cab of No 65441 is seen from the platform at Cambridge on 6 July 1957.

And how many railway enthusiasts started the same way as these two on the platform? Also at Cambridge in June 1957, where a Class E4 2-4-0 is waiting, possibly on a Mildenhall train, with the driver enjoying a joke with his mate. And the real heart of the matter – the fireman on the footplate of Class J15 No 65469, at Norwich City on the occasion of the commemorative run to Norwich Thorpe on 21 May 1960. Electric trains are *much* faster and cleaner, but . . .
John Brodribb collection/A. R. J. Frost/A. J. Willmott

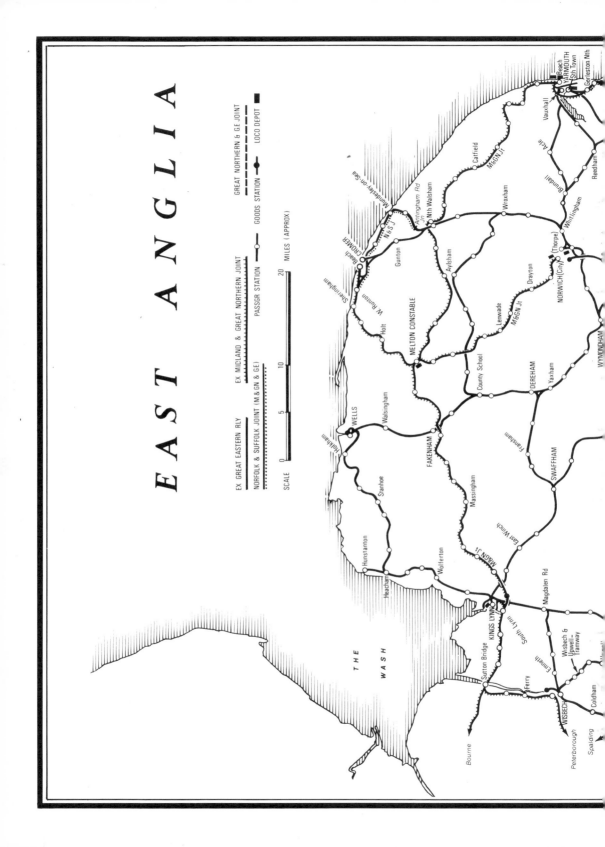

EAST ANGLIA

EX GREAT EASTERN RLY

EX MIDLAND & GREAT NORTHERN JOINT

NORFOLK & SUFFOLK JOINT (M & GN & GE)

GREAT NORTHERN & GE JOINT

PASSGR STATION ⊸

GOODS STATION ⬥

LOCO DEPOT ■

SCALE

0   5   10   20

MILES (APPROX)

THE WASH

Hunstanton
Heacham
Wolferton
Snettisham
M&GN Jt
KINGS LYNN
South Lynn
Magdalen Rd
Sutton Bridge
Emneth
Ferry
Wisbech & Upwell Tramway
WISBECH
Coldham
Bourne
Peterborough
Spalding

Wells
Holkham
Walsingham
Stanhoe
FAKENHAM
Massingham
East Winch
SWAFFHAM

Sheringham
Beach CROMER
W Runton
Holt
MELTON CONSTABLE
County School
DEREHAM
Yaxham
Fransham
WYMONDHAM

Mundesley-on-Sea
Antingham Rd Jn
N & S J
Gunton
Nth Walsham
Aylsham
Lenwade
Drayton
M&GN Jt
NORWICH (City)
(Thorpe)
Catfield
M&GN Jt
Wroxham

Beach
YARMOUTH Sth Town
Gorleston Nth
Vauxhall
Acle
Reedham
Ilepuna
Whitlingham
Buckenham